Crime and Criminals
in Victorian Lincolnshire

A PUBLIC DINNER.

CRIME AND CRIMINALS
IN VICTORIAN LINCOLNSHIRE

by

ADRIAN GRAY, M.A.

PAUL WATKINS
STAMFORD
1993

Published by
PAUL WATKINS
18, Adelaide Street,
Stamford,
Lincolnshire, PE9 2EN.

ISBN
1 871615 43 7

Photoset from the discs of the author by
Paul Watkins (Publishing)

Printed and bound by Woolnoughs of Irthlingborough.

CONTENTS

THE FIVE WADMEN IN THE WORKHOUSE.

For Rita Jones

LIST OF ILLUSTRATIONS

The reproductions of contemporary woodcuts are from *The Burning Shame, or Morality Alarmed in this Neighbourhood*, a contemporary childrens' book in the possession of the author. The illustrations from *The Trial of Sir Jasper* and *Illustrated Temperance Anecdotes* are from copies in the possession of the publisher. Miscellaneous small decorations are from Victorian books in the possession of the publisher.

ix

PRELUDE

The Victorian age is now nearly a century ago, but it is one that is still familiar to us today due to frequent portrayals of it on television and through the classic literature of the period. However, such depictions show only a few aspects of a long, rich and complex era — and they tell us relatively little about what life was really like for the ordinary folk of Victorian Lincolnshire.

To modern readers, the legal system of the Victorian period may seem harsh and vindictive — as it often actually was. But it is also important to remember that, when Queen Victoria ascended the throne in 1837, the country was already benefitting from the liberal reform of the criminal code made by Sir Robert Peel while he was Home Secretary in the early 1820s. These reforms included the abolition of the death penalty for many offences.

Nonetheless the shadow of the harsh and draconian past cast a deep gloom over Victorian Lincolnshire. Public execution and transportation were a feature of the legal system until the middle of the period, and anyone who fell foul of the law could still be terrified by tales of what had happened to people like Tom Otter...

In 1805, during the repressive days of the Napoleonic Wars, Tom Otter was something of a rake and a ne'er do well in Lincolnshire. Although he was commonly believed to have a wife tucked away in some obscure cottage, Otter was a constant threat to the chastity and good name of local peasant girls. One of these succumbed to his charms rather too enthusiastically, and in the due course of time a baby was born.

Today such occurrences would hardly attract any official attention whatsoever, but for Tom Otter they meant trouble. An unmarried mother and child were likely to become a burden on the local poor rates, a tax from which needy cases were supported. The law allowed for some duress to be placed upon errant fathers, and Tom Otter was made to marry the unfortunate young woman — the authorities being ignorant as to his marital status! Thus Otter was married in Hykeham church, with a parish constable on either side of him.

Forcing two people to marry was hardly likely to bring about wedded bliss, and so it proved with Otter. The evening of his wedding, he murdered his bride with a hedge stake as they were walking along a lane near Harby.

Such a crude murder with an obvious suspect needed little detective work. Otter was caught, tried, and sentenced to death. He was hanged at Lincoln, then his body was encased in pitch, fastened in irons and hung from a gibbet. His remains were put on public display near the Fosse Dyke, on the road from Lincoln to Gainsborough, close to the Drinsey Nook public house. A local lane became known as 'Tom Otter's Lane.'

Otter's remains became a regular attraction for people with little to do on Sunday afternoons. For the first few weeks the exhibition drew large crowds, but gradually interest faded. Birds built a nest in the skull and local people made up a rhyme or riddle:

The living dwell within the dead
The old go out to fetch in bread
To feed the young within the head.

Though the body fell apart, the gibbet post survived into the Victorian period as the last of a bygone era. It fell down in 1850 and Lincoln tradesmen made pieces of it into souvenirs.

Otter's story is a fitting prelude to the Victorian age as it reveals the harsh authoritarianism that was then common. Yet it should also be known that Otter was not alone when he was hanged — beside him died David Dickensen, convicted and sentenced to death for the crime of stealing a sheep.

Adrian Gray
Ruskington, *April 1993*

xi

John Tenniel.]   [Butterworth & Heath.

‘ See the degraded wretch we picture here :
He blights the corn before it reach the ear.’

xii

Charles Mercier.]   [Butterworth & Heath.

'ENTER THE PRISON: see the good man there,
Who from the death-doomed sinner drives despair.'

H. Anelay.]   [Butterworth & Heath.

'And when the babe was dead,
'Twas 'accidental death' the jury said.'

xiv

CHAPTER ONE: WILFUL MURDER

'Wilful murder' was the most serious offence under the Victorian criminal code and carried an automatic death sentence, though in many cases this was commuted to transportation or life imprisonment. Murder exercised a powerful hold over the imagination of all classes. They perhaps took their cue from Charles Dickens, who loved to revisit the scenes of murders and terrify his friends with the details. The spread of newspapers during the period contributed a great deal to this; notable murders were reported in great detail in every paper across the country.

1. The Poisoners

The 'classic' Victorian murder was always a poisoning. One of the reasons for this was that a number of highly dangerous substances were easily available from chemists for poisoning rats, which were endemic in many Victorian households. Poison was easy to use and seems to have appealed especially to female murderers, who generally slipped a little into their victim's tea or dinner.

An interesting case that combined two factors guaranteed to scare the Victorian gentry occurred in Lincoln in 1838. The dangers of poison were well known, but there was also an awareness of the dangers of rebellious servants, a fear which reached its peak in 1840, with the celebratedly bloody murder of Lord William Russell in London by his own butler. In the Lincoln case, fifteen-year-old Samuel Kirkby was accused of having murdered John Bruce, a highly-respected local butcher.

John Bruce was taken very ill soon after eating his breakfast and died only a few hours later. Medical evidence at the coroner's inquest proved that he had died from arsenic poisoning and Samuel Kirkby, an apprentice to Bruce, was charged with having put the arsenic in the tea kettle.

As can be imagined, the consequences of putting arsenic in the kettle could have been disastrous for the whole household. Bruce was killed by it, but a servant girl called Susan Quincey and another woman, Elizabeth Raven, both survived despite being violently ill.

PC Thomas Ashton had little difficulty arresting Kirkby, a lad who seems to have been filled with foolish bravado. 'I suppose you will go to all the druggists of the town,' he told the policeman. 'If you do, you'll not find anything out.'

Kirkby's belief in his own cleverness was misplaced. He had got the arsenic (or 'white mercury' as it was often called) from a younger boy named William Hicks, who ran errands for a chemist named Mr Bottle. Kirkby maintained that he had put the white mercury, which was used as a rat killer, down the privy. However, witnesses came forward to say that Mr Bruce had flogged Kirkby a few days before his death, and that the apprentice had wished his master dead.

Kirkby's trial at the Summer Assize lasted eight hours, but the jury took only twenty minutes to reach a verdict of Guilty. The judge read out the mandatory sentence of death, which seemed to have little effect on Kirkby who 'retained the same firmness he had exhibited during the course of his trial, his features unaltering in the slightest degree.'

Due to the boy's age, petitions were raised in his favour and his sentence was altered to one of transportation for life. Kirkby then freely confessed his guilt, saying that he had put poison in the tea kettle and the cream jug. He was visited in Lincoln gaol by his father, then taken to the Green Man public house as the first step of his journey to Woolwich and on for transportation. At the public house, young Kirkby asked for a glass of grog and a cigar just like any other stagecoach passenger. On the way to Woolwich, 'he laughed and grimaced... and said that now his head was out of the hemp he did not care for what might come.'

Kirkby was undoubtedly a wicked and vindictive boy, but it can be assumed that his murderous revenge resulted in a number of masters being rather more considerate to their apprentices.

One of the most infamous poisoners of Victorian Lincolnshire was the detested Barnetby poisoner, Mary Ann Milner. In June 1847 the small village of Barnetby-le-Wold was rocked by the death of three of its people, and the dangerous illness of at least one other, all of whom were rumoured to have been poisoned. The news became all the more sensational when it was reported that the daughter- in-law of one of the dead people had been arrested on a charge of wilful murder.

Mary Ann Milner, a young woman of 27, seems to have been motivated by a mixture of greed, spite and frustration. The first of her victims to die was her mother-in-law, Mary Milner, whose husband was also poisoned, though he survived; it seems likely in this case that Mary Ann Milner was motivated by the prospect of financial gain and the improvement of her own living conditions. The second fatal victim was another woman from the village, who seems to have been killed for no reason other than that the poisoner disliked her.

In July 1847 Mary Ann Milner appeared at Lincoln Assizes on a charge of wilfully murdering her mother-in-law. The dead woman and her husband had become very ill on 2nd June; the woman had died, while her husband lost the use of his right side though he remained alive. Although some symptoms of poisoning were evident, Mrs Milner had been buried before suspicions became clear enough for her to be exhumed and examined in closer detail. Arsenic was found in her stomach.

William Percival, a Barnetby shopkeeper, gave evidence that he had sold arsenic to Mary Ann Milner. He remembered joking with her that arsenic was a difficult thing for him to sell but that as she was clearly not suicidal he did not need to worry. However, he advised her to buy some antimonical wince as an antidote, and Mary Milner told him that her dog had once died from eating rat poison. It was alleged that the young woman had then included the arsenic in her recipe for sage and gruel that she dished up for her in-laws.

It was argued that the motive was financial gain. Both the older Milners had savings in a burial club (a form of life insurance that also covered the cost of funerals), and just after her mother-in-law died Mary Ann withdrew £5 from her account, part of which she used to buy mourning materials.

Despite this strong evidence, there was nothing to show that the young woman had given the poison to the old couple. Victorian juries were very reluctant to convict in a murder case if there was any element of doubt, and here there was no real proof of who had put the arsenic in the food. Mary Ann Milner received a verdict of Not Guilty, only to be immediately put back on trial for the murder of Hannah Jickels.

Hannah Jickels was a neighbour of Milner whose child died on 15th June with many of the symptoms of having been poisoned. Mrs Jickels herself died on 26th June but, unlike the other victims, gave a clear indication of the source of her violent illness before she died.

Mrs Jickels had been seen around in good spirits on 26th June and was invited to have a breakfast of pancakes with Mary Ann Milner. Later in the morning she went back to her own house and fell onto her knees, vomiting strongly. She told Mary Winter that she had been poisoned by some pancakes given to her by Milner, and Mrs Winter helped her upstairs to bed. There the sick woman was hardly able to speak, but complained that her throat and mouth were very hot; she was very thirsty and in great agony.

An Account of the Trial, conviction and Condemnation of M. Ann Milner, at Lincoln Assizes July

20th, 1847 for the Murder of Hannah Jickells at Barnetby le-Wold.

Mary Ann Milner, aged 27, was charged with having wilfully murdered Mary Milner at Barnetby-le-Wold in the parts of Lindsey, by administering a quantity of arsenic. After a very long trial of six hours, his Lordship summed up, when the jury consulted for a few minutes and returned a verdict of not guilty.

The prisoner was then arranged under a second indictment charged with the murder of Hannah Jickells, on the 20th of June, by administering poison.

Mary the wife of William Winter said she lived under the same roof as the deceased although in a separate house. She saw the deceased on the 25th of June who was in good health at that time ; in the evening deceased went to Kettleby, and the prisoner who was her sister-in-law went into her house to her husband, she remarked it because it was a strange occurrence—next morning she saw the deceased who was in good health, at about half-past 8, and saw her again at 10. She afterwards went into her house and found her down upon her knees vomiting violently, and declaring she was poisoned by eating pancakes at the prisoner's. Witness held her head, afterwards she assisted her up stairs where she continued very sick—she was so weak as scarcely to be able to speak, but complained of her throat and mouth, which she said were very hot ; she was thirsty and appeared in great agony, as she frequently threw herself up and down the bed—she asked for her husband and he came home at about 1 o'clock—saw the prisoner at about half-past two o'clock and said "Hannah Jickells has been eating pancakes along with you and has been poisoned with them". Prisoner turned white but made no answer. She then told her that deceased said so. Eliz Thompson was by at the time this was said. Witness then went to deceased's bed-room followed by prisoner. deceased was throwing up very violently, prisoner said to her "do you think I would put anything into the cakes and poison you ?" deceased made no answer—she asked deceased if she had taken anything herself, deceased replied she never had any poison in her house. She several times declared she should die as she had been poisoned by eating the pancakes—deceased died at 6 o'clock that evening. She (the witness) ordered her daughter to throw away that which the deceased had thrown up into a wash tub, her daughter did so. the deceased also threw up in some other vessels, and she ordered that to be saved for the surgeons to analyze, and particularly told the prisoner not to throw it away ; it was however thrown away and upon asking the prisoner why it was thrown away, she replied it was offensive to the room ; the vessels were well, cleaned out. Prisoner was in the room when the deceased died, and remarked that she died like her poor mother Milner and deceased's child which had died on the 15th of June. On the day deceased died the prisoner came to her house and said that as the deceased had no fire would she have some pancakes with her at her house for breakfast, she (the prisoner) had had some, and could easily try another for deceased. deceased said she was very fond of them, she had been thinking of frying herself one but had no eggs, and would therefore go to prisoner's house.—The prisoner at the same time said, "Hannah does not blame me in the least for putting anything into the cakes."

Elizabeth Winter the daughter of Mary Winter, remembered the day of deceased's death ; saw her in the morning of that day in the garden, she was in good health and spirits at that time it was 9 o'clock ; saw the wash-tub and emptied it, there was something like bread or pancake in it with phlegm, she threw it on the ash hill, and afterwards pointed out what she had thrown there, to some men who took it up.

William Booth, a shoemaker in company with G. Watson, searched a dunghil and was shewn by Elizabeth Winter, a quantity of matter, which he delivered to the constable Mackerell.

Constable Mackerell received the matter and gave it to the coroner and afterwards to Messrs. Patteson and Moxon.

Wm. Percival a shop-keeper at Barnetby-le-Wold knew the prisoner ; sold her 2 oz. of arsenic when she applied for it, he said it was an awkward sort of thing to sell, but as she was not a person likely to kill herself he did not object. She said she wanted it to kill mice, and that the dog got that which she before had, and he died in the most excruciating agony. He recommended the untimonical wine for the deceased.

Mr. James Burdett Moxon, a surgeon residing at Glandford Brigg, attended the deceased and found her vomiting and purging, she was so weak she seldom spoke, but complained of pain in her stomach. He was suspicious of poison at first seeing her. Prisoner and her mother Sarah Jickels were in the room. He asked the prisoner a question relative to the cause of the deceased's illness, the prisoner said she had had some pancakes with her, he examined the matter which the deceased vomited and it looked like partly digested food. He applied several tests all with similar results, which quite satisfied him that arsenic was in the stomach to the amount of 30 grains : 10 or 12 grains was quite sufficient to kill any person, 4 grains had been known to kill a person.

Mr. Milner made a very eloquent appeal on behalf of the prisoner, and the Judge summoned up, dividing the evidence into sections. The Jury must be convinced that the deceased died from the effects of poison, and his lordship then read over, and commented upon, the evidence of the surgeons. The next question was how was it administered and recapitulated the evidence relative to the cake, and then, if the poison was administered in the cake, was it done by the prisoner, she intending to murder the deceased —upon all these points the jury must satisfy themselves and return the verdict according to the evidence.

The jury consulted for some minutes and then returned a verdict of Guilty.

During the whole trial the prisoner remained firm and collected, nor did her demeanor alter when the jury returned their verdict, or when his lordship passed sentence.

In passing sentence his lordship alluded to the dreadful crime of murder, and said he confessed he almost felt to tremble for the security of our lives, and of the continuance of trial by jury, if the gentlemen had came to any other conclusion than the one they had just expressed, after the careful and minute sitting of the evidence : for how many other murders she might have committed it was not for them to determine, for her crimes she would have to seek intercession for mercy with her Maker. She seduced her unfortunate victim under her roof to partake of her hospitality, and in the face of one of her children administered to her poison and sent her to her long account. It was hardly necessary in this case to say that on this side the grave she need not hope for mercy, and advised her to employ the time she had to live, in seeking instruction which would assist in reconciling her with that God whose laws she had so outrageously violated. His lordship then in a very solemn tone of voice sentenced the prisoner to Death.

R. E. Leary, Printer, 19 Strait, Lincoln.

The broadside describing the trial of Ann Milner
Lincolnshire Public Libraries

4

In the early afternoon Mrs Winter went to see Mary Ann Milner and told her that Mrs Jickels declared she had been poisoned by Milner's pancakes, a statement which was also witnessed by Elizabeth Thompson. Mary Ann Milner turned white but said nothing, but later in the afternoon visited the stricken woman's bedside.

'Do you think I would put anything into the cakes and poison you?' Mrs Milner had asked, but the dying woman had said nothing. However, she later repeated her allegations about the pancakes and James Moxon, a surgeon from Brigg, suspected poison as soon as he saw her.

Various evidence was collected and given to Moxon. Unfortunately Mrs Jickels had first been sick in a wash-tub and this had been cleaned out by Mrs Winter's daughter who had seen something like pancake in it; however the girl threw the contents onto an ash-hill and these were later collected up for the evidence by a local shoemaker. Mrs Winter asked her daughter to keep some of the vomit that was in other containers, but when Mary Ann Milner visited the house she cleaned them out and said this was because they were 'offensive.'

Moxon examined the remains from the ash-hill and found that they were partly-digested pancake. By testing them and the remaining contents of the dead woman's stomach, he estimated that Mrs Jickels had been given 30 grains of arsenic; 12 were enough to kill a person.

Although no real motive seems to have been established, there seemed to be strong evidence that Mrs Jickels had died from eating the poisoned pancakes. Mary Ann Milner was found guilty and sentenced to be hanged on 30th July 1847, an event which excited great curiosity throughout the county. A crowd of thousands gathered on the appointed morning, only to receive shattering news: Mary Ann Milner had cheated the gallows by hanging herself with a handkerchief in her own cell during the night. The matron of the prison was asked to explain why female prisoners who were awaiting execution were left unattended the night before their appointment with eternity, and seemed rather surprised that anyone should even be interested.

Cases of deliberate poisoning did not always end in verdicts of guilty to a charge of wilful murder. Insanity or youth were often taken as mitigating factors and, in such cases, manslaughter was more likely to be the verdict. In 1862 a 13-year-old nursemaid, Elizabeth Vamplew, was arrested for poisoning a farmer's baby daughter at Alvingham near Louth. Although she had obviously made a deliberate decision to kill the child, her extreme youth and obvious confusion suggested that wilful murder was an inappropriate description of her act.

In July 1862 Kate Taylor, a ten-week-old baby, died suddenly after a period of ill-health. The main symptoms were a frothing at the mouth, twitching and sweating; a local woman commented before the death that the child had been dosed with 'sleeping stuff,' by which she may have meant laudanum, still in common use at the time.

Elizabeth Vamplew was suspected immediately, as she had complained that she was 'tired of lugging the thing about.' There was strong evidence against her: the baby's stomach contained strychnine, one of the main ingredients of 'Battle's Vermin Killer' which Vamplew used regularly on her own hair. The girl also admitted to giving the child white mercury.

At her trial, Vamplew was a pitiful spectacle. When asked how she pleaded on a charge of wilful murder, she replied 'Guilty' and then became very confused. After consultations, she was allowed to change her plea to Not Guilty. This allowed a verdict of guilty to the lesser charge of manslaughter to be brought in and she received a sentence of twelve years' penal servitude. The jury requested that the Home Secretary should be advised of the dangers of various commercial brands of vermin powder.

2. Insanity and Instability

In Victorian Britain much was still to be learnt about mental illness and a number of murders occurred where mental illness was an evident factor. On 7th October 1850 George Sinderson was murdered by Robert Meggitt at Bonby, a fairly typical example of the cases that could occur.

Meggitt was an old man of 73 who was said to have been 'odd in the head' since he had been on a journey to Essex and fallen from a cart. He lived with his wife in the same house as George Sinderson, the Meggitts sleeping downstairs and the others upstairs. According to Meggitt, Sinderson treated him badly and threatened to 'shake him to death.'

Other witnesses stated that the old man's behaviour was often dangerous. On the night of the murder he suddenly started rushing about the house 'in a crazed way' with a pair of tongs, threatening to 'smash someone's brains out.' People in the house managed to get the tongs off Meggitt and someone ran for help while Sinderson held the old man down. However, Meggitt suddenly struck Sinderson with a knife which he had concealed, as a result of which Sinderson died.

Meggitt was arrested for wilful murder but as he was not considered to be in his right mind a verdict of not guilty was recorded. He was instead ordered to be detained.

A confusing case where disability was clearly an issue arose over the murder of a village schoolmistress at Quadring, near Spalding, in 1842. Miss Mary Spencer, aged 40, lived in a cottage just off the turnpike road, and pupils came to her for lessons there. One Friday morning the scholars arrived to find the blinds still down. As the door was unlocked, one or two ventured to look inside, and found a dreadful scene. The floors, wall and furniture were spattered with blood and the body of Miss Spencer lay with its head half-severed.

News of the brutal murder spread rapidly through the district and the scene was discussed by a Mr Loughland, a land surveyor, with a friend. He was overheard by a labourer called Hewitt, who commented, 'I wonder what Bill's been up to. He was out all night and came home covered in blood.'

Hewitt's son was soon arrested and most of the details of the case had been collected together by the time the inquest was held at the Brown Cow Inn. Bill Hewitt, aged 22, was a 'very good looking' and powerful man, who was both deaf and dumb. His family seems to have tried to tell the truth, reporting that he came home late on the night of the murder and acted in a disturbed or frightened manner. He changed his clothes, getting rid of a blue smock, and attempted to wash a white shirt himself rather than letting his mother do it. The shirt was found by a policeman between his mattress and the bed with blood marks on it.

Through an interpreter, Hewitt explained that he'd got drunk and had had a nosebleed, which he used as the explanation for bloody marks found on his knife. He claimed to have seen a 'man with a bundle' pass Miss Spencer's house on the Thursday night, and to have been frightened by a mysterious stranger outside his own house. However, the Coroner's court recorded that Miss Spencer had been murdered and Hewitt was taken to Lincoln gaol.

What was unclear was the reason for Miss Spencer's death. Hewitt died of tuberculosis whilst still in prison, so the extent by which he was hampered through his disabilities was never made clear. It was reported, however, that he had had dinner at Miss Spencer's house during the fateful week. The full story, however, must remain a mystery.

A case that nearly ended in the same way occurred in Ruskington in April 1862. Henry Newton, a young tailor who was described as 'an imbecile' and 'not rational', lived with his aunt and her family. One day, without any apparent reason, he followed his cousin Louisa Barr into the wash-house and attempted to cut her throat with a knife. Louisa screamed, and was rescued by a Mr Tomlinson before the mad youth could inflict any more damage on her than surface cuts on her neck and thumb. Although he was tried for attempted murder, Newton was also found not guilty for reasons of insanity and subsequently was detained.

3. Murderous Thieves and other Violent Deaths
A number of Victorian murders were motivated by theft, ending in death either through careless misjudgment of the degree of violence or in a desperate attempt to escape capture.

A typical case was the attack on farmer Parker of Ingleby in December 1842. Parker had been to Lincoln fat stock market during the day and returned home with a fair sum of money. That evening he went out to a lecture at Saxilby church, probably with the money still on him, but was found at the roadside with a head wound. The farmer died that night, leaving six orphan children, but his assailant was never caught. It seems that this was a routine type of highway robbery where the disabling blow proved fatal.

Saxilby people were still living in terror of murderous thieves when, the very next month, rumours swept around that a local woman had been murdered in her bed! This case involved 90-year-old Fanny Harrison, who had been woken by the sound of an intruder at 2am. The man put a hand across her mouth and struck her across the wrist with a poker, but her screams of 'Murder!' awakened neighbours and the thief ran off across the fields. Mrs Harrison was found dead, but it turned out that she had died of fright rather than been struck down by a murderer.

Another bizarre case of a robbery that went wrong occurred at Croft, between Wainfleet and Skegness, in February 1843. Elderly Elizabeth Evinson lived with her sister, Ann Fairweather, in a cottage beside the road between the two towns, a situation always likely to encourage unwelcome visitors. One Sunday night at about 10 o'clock a man forced his way in through a window and tied the two old women to an iron bedstead while he ransacked their cottage for its few valuables. He then threw the bedclothes over the women so they could see nothing, and made his escape.

The two women remained fixed to the bed until Tuesday morning, when a neighbour heard Ann Fairweather's cries for help. By this stage Mrs Evinson had died and so a murder hunt began.

A few days later a man was arrested at Swineshead on a charge of passing counterfeit coin and a search of him revealed a number of silver spoons that matched those missing from the house at Croft. Thomas Johnson was tried for murder and on 28th March 1843 was sentenced to death, his execution taking place at Lincoln Castle on 5th April. Perhaps it is surprising that Johnson was found guilty of wilful murder and he was surely one of the few murderers whose chosen weapon was a bedstead.

Another case with a strange twist involved the murder of Charles Copeman at Kirton-in-Lindsey on 19th December 1847. Copeman, from Blyborough, was a victim of a particularly vicious highway robber. Joseph Travis was arrested for the crime and brought to the Assize on a charge of wilful murder. However, there was insufficient evidence to prove the capital charge and Travis was acquitted.

A woodcut of the Lincoln gallows, from a broadside of 1831
Lincolnshire Libraries

Soon afterwards Lincolnshire was shocked by the news that a man who had actually seen Travis murder Copeman had come forward. This was a bricklayer who had been asleep at the time and had been awoken by the noise of the murder. Travis had bribed the bricklayer to stay silent and promised him £2 if he was acquitted, but then reneged on the bargain. When the bricklayer had complained, Travis had warned him that accepting bribes was also a serious offence. Nonetheless the man came forward with his evidence.

Once Travis had been acquitted of murder, he could not be put on trial again. Instead he was charged with highway robbery, stealing four sovereigns and 7s. 6d. from Charles Copeman. This time the verdict went against him and Travis was sentenced to life transportation. He had escaped the hangman and felt able to confess to the murder as well.

4. Murder in the Family

The statement that most murders are committed by people who know the victim was as true in Victorian times as it is today. Out of eighteen people who were executed in Lincoln during the period (including one who committed suicide first), no fewer than twelve murdered a relative or girlfriend. Perhaps typical was John Ward, aged 26, who killed his own mother with a shotgun as she had interfered with his relationship with a servant girl, Susan Bogg. He put up a weak defence — that the shotgun had fired accidentally — but huge crowds turned up on 27th July 1849 to watch his execution by hangman Calcraft, who was paid £5 with an option to keep the victim's clothes. Ward bounded up the steps to the scaffold two at a time. Incidentally, the executioner was paid £6 if his victim was a woman.

A wife-murderer who escaped the hangman was William Lilburn, on the grounds that he had been pressured into the deed by his mother. Lilburn was a pipemaker and cow-keeper who lived at Waterside, Lincoln. The key witness was a neighbour named Mary Smith, who described the prelude to the events of 27th September 1842 and the events of the day itself in great detail. She said she had often heard Lilburn's mother, an old nurse, telling him to give his wife a good beating and the old woman had even told another neighbour that her daughter-in-law 'ought to be gibbetted.'

Evidence was given to show the dead woman had been stable and of good character until her marriage in about 1837, after which she took to drink and began taking laudanum. Mary Smith was close by when the young woman received the fatal blow from a 'camerel,' which the old lady tried to persuade her to take away. When she refused, it was hidden in the house instead.

Someone tipped the police off about what was happening, but it was too late to save the younger Mrs Lilburn, who died following bleeding from the mouth. Police watched as the old woman poured a basin of blood into the gutter, before going off to get a Burial Certificate only two hours after the poor woman had died. She gave cause of death as a burst blood vessel.

Lilburn was arrested and charged with wilful murder as he had struck the fatal blow, his mother being charged as an accessory. Given her role in the affair, he was sentenced to only ten years' transportation and despatched to Woolwich. However, in January 1846 Lilburn informed the authorities of an escape attempt and received a free pardon.

A long and complex case involved Thomas Bacon from Stamford. In January 1857 Bacon was arrested for cutting the throats of his own children while living in London, and his wife — who had spent some time in an asylum — was also arrested. Orders were also made to exhume the body of Bacon's mother, who had died in Stamford in May 1855 and had been buried at Great Casterton. It was suspected that she had been poisoned by him.

Thomas and Mrs Bacon were tried for the London murders in May 1857 but Thomas was acquitted while his wife was found to be guilty, though clearly mentally ill. Bacon was immediately despatched to Lincoln where he was tried for murdering his own mother by putting arsenic in her broth. Although *The Observer* reported that Mrs Bacon had admitted to poisoning her mother-in-law, Bacon went on trial in Lincoln. However, the charge of wilful murder was dropped as the passage of time made much of the evidence unclear, but Bacon was found guilty of administering arsenic with intent to murder. He thus escaped the hangman but not the prison cell, bringing to an end a particularly sordid and sorrowful case.

The conviction did not please everyone, because Bacon's guilt had already been established in numerous pamphlets and broadsides. There were also several contemporary ballads written. One such contained a particularly gruesome illustration, reproduced on the next page. The picture is misleading because Bacon's daughter was only 11 months old when she was murdered.

Contemporary woodcut of the gruesome deed of Thomas Bacon.
From the Phillips Collection, Stamford.

Another poisoner was Priscilla Biggadyke of Mareham-le-Fen, whose husband Richard died on 1st October 1868. Richard Biggadyke was a well-sinker and earned a reasonable living from which he supported his wife and their three children, and they added to their income by taking in two lodgers. He was poisoned by his wife adding chemicals to his tea, though she blamed one of the lodgers, Procter. However, evidence was produced to show that the marriage had turned sour.

In court she made a strange spectacle:

> The prisoner would be considered a good looking woman but for the smallness of her eyes, which give one an impression of great determination. She is thick-set and about 5ft 2ins in height. She was meanly attired, and her straw bonnet had evidently seen much service.

This humble appearance failed to save her from the scaffold and she was the first person to be executed at Lincoln under the Private Executions Act.

The tomb of Ann Bacon at Great Casterton

On 19th December 1893 Henry Rumbell, captain of a Grimsby fishing smack, was executed for the murder of Harriet Rushby, who would nowadays be described as his 'live-in lover,' though the cause of the murder seems to have been that she did too little living-in and rather too much loving-out.

Rumbell had set up house with Harriet Rushby in Stanley Street, but decided to make alternative arrangements for when he went away on a lengthy fishing trip. He arranged for Harriet to stay at a relative's house in Ayscoughe Street, for which Rumbell would pay the expenses; this suggests that he did not trust his 'partner' when she was on her own.

On 7th November, after more than two weeks away, Rumbell came back and went straight to his relative's house. He discovered that Harriet had not even been there once, so in a fury he went to a gunsmith's shop and bought a revolver and fifty rounds.

13

At 8.40pm Rumbell called on Ann Widall, who told him that Harriet had gone with a Mr and Mrs Bowdidge and another man to the Empire Music Hall, thus confirming all Rumbell's worst fears. However, he met Harriet and Mrs Bowdidge in Cleethorpes Road, so together they went to the Exchange public house and then to the Music Hall.

Rumbell discovered that Harriet had been living with Mrs Bowdidge in Tunnard Street, and persuaded her to go back there with him. The two were in a downstairs room when Mrs Bowdidge returned with the 'other man,' Burns, the lodger. By this stage Rumbell and Harriet Rushby were well into a quarrel over whether she had 'been with' other men. 'You have deceived me and no other man shall have you,' Rumbell shouted, 'you shall not leave this place alive.'

He then forced her to go upstairs while the others seem to have stood around doing very little. As he climbed the stairs, Rumbell turned back and spoke to Burns. 'If we don't meet in this world we shall in the next,' he said.

The audience downstairs heard Harriet scream, 'Don't murder me in my sins!' There were then two shots. Soon after, Rumbell came downstairs covered with blood. He asked for his hat and left, Burns apparently making no attempt to intervene.

Rumbell told his landlord what he had done and was persuaded to give himself up. He surrendered his revolver to a policeman but this did not atone for the committing of the murder and he was sentenced to death. Rumbell's last request to the judge was for a supply of cigars while he awaited execution.

In the condemned cell Rumbell was visited several times by the Bishop of Lincoln. He was quite cheerful about his fate and expressed the view that he would be meeting Harriet in the next world, where all would be fine.

USEFUL SUNDAY LITERATURE FOR THE MASSES;

OR, MURDER MADE FAMILIAR.

Father of a Family (reads). "The wretched Murderer is supposed to have cut the throats of his three eldest Children, and then to have killed the Baby by beating it repeatedly with a Poker. * * * * * In person he is of a rather bloated appearance, with a bull neck, small eyes, broad large nose, and coarse vulgar mouth. His dress was a light blue coat, with brass buttons, elegant yellow summer vest, and pepper-and-salt trowsers. When at the Station House he expressed himself as being rather 'peckish,' and said he should like a Black Pudding, which, with a Cup of Coffee, was immediately procured for him."

The popularity of murder literature satirised by *Punch* in 1849.

5. A Catalogue of Murderers

Given below is a list of all those executed at Lincoln during the Victorian era. The last to be executed in public, at Lincoln Castle, were Dickett and Carey in 1859, whose demise was watched by a crowd estimated at 20,000. From 1868 all executions were done in private, generally with only about four people present. This was the era when the famous executioner Calcraft gave way to Marwood, who had started his career as a Horncastle shoemaker!

17th March 1843: *Thomas Johnson*, for murder of an old woman at Croft

2nd August 1844: *Eliza Joyce*, for child murder at Boston

30th July 1847: *Mary Ann Milner*, who escaped execution by committing suicide

27th July 1849: *John Ward*, for murder of his mother

5th August 1859: *William Pickett* (20) and *Henry Carey* (24) for murder of William Stevensen near Sibsey

28th December 1868: *Priscilla Biggadyke*, who poisoned her husband at Mareham-le-Fen

1st April 1872: *William Horry*, for wife murder at Boston

9th August 1875: *Peter Blanchard*, murdered his sweetheart at Louth on 7th March 1875

29th March 1877: *William Clarke*, a poacher who killed a gamekeeper at Norton Disney on 30th January

19th February 1883: *James Anderson*, for wife murder at East Ferry

7th May 1883: *Thomas Garry*, for murder of J. Newton at Great Hale

26th May 1884: *Mary Lefley*, poisoned her husband at Wrangle

21st February 1887: *Richard Insole*, wife murder at Grimsby

28th July 1891: *Arthur Spencer*, murdered Mary Garner at Lincoln

19th December 1893: *Henry Rumbell*, murdered Harriet Rushby at Grimsby

27th July 1897: *Joseph Bowser*, for wife murder at Donington Northorpe

25th July 1899: *Edward Bell*, for wife murder at Weston

A contemporary postcard of William Marwood's portrait, cobbler's shop and visiting card. An original can be seen at Lincolnshire Police Museum

CHAPTER TWO: CRIMES OF VIOLENCE

There are some people who argue that society is getting more violent but in Victorian England, when the population was much smaller than today, the courts were often crowded with those who had hit, stabbed or bashed, often under the influence of alcohol or bad temper or both.

Sometimes violent behaviour ended in death and could even involve 'respectable' members of society. Edward Richardson, accused of manslaughter at Reepham in November 1855, was a farmer with an annual income of £600. The victim, Henry Blow, was a young farm labourer who worked for a man named Mason who had decided to sell up and leave. After the sale, Mason was joined at his house by a few friends including Edward Richardson and his son Thomas.

Clearly Mason's decision to sell up created some resentment among his labourers because they were likely to lose their jobs. Half an hour after midnight stones were thrown at his house and several panes of glass cracked, but the farmers gathered inside burst out with sticks in their hands and surprised Henry Blow and three others who had spent an evening imbibing alcohol.

Blow and the others were taken into Mason's house as suspects and a fight soon broke out. During this one of the labourers was cut on the head and Blow was knocked down senseless. However, five minutes later Blow got up and began fighting again. When he left for home, the house 'looked like a butcher's shop.' Blow died a few hours later and was found to have a fractured skull. Though there was much argument over whether the fatal blow had been struck by the Richardsons or caused by Blow falling over while drunk, the case clearly showed how drunken violence could be endemic in any village.

Manslaughter cases resulted in widely different sentences. A case at Leake in 1867 resulted in a sentence of only two months for Frederick White, who had killed William Davison. Davison and White had been on good terms until the latter challenged the former to a fight when in the public house on 25th October. Davison was reluctant to join in but White hit him several times with a cripple's crutch. Although Davison did not seem badly injured at the time, he died soon afterwards of a ruptured abdomen.

Another serious offence was attempted murder. This included cases of poisonings that failed to achieve their objectives, such as the offence committed by seventeen-year-old Sarah Digby at West Deeping in 1868. This was an interesting — and bizarre — example of a crime committed by a servant girl against her mistress.

Sarah Digby was one of several servants employed by Mrs Mary Smith, who also had some daughters of her own. Sarah stole £5 from Mrs Smith's workbox, but the lady did not know which member of the household had taken it. To frighten one of them into confessing, she declared that she was going to visit an old fenland 'wise woman' who would show her the face of the thief in a glass.

This ruse was believed by Sarah Digby but her reaction was not what Mrs Smith would have expected. She decided to use Blade's Rat & Mouse Poison to kill her mistress, by putting it in her broth and tea. However, she did not put enough in to kill Mrs Smith, who became suspicious when she saw a white paste at the bottom of her tea cup. Sarah Digby received a sentence of ten years' penal servitude.

Drunks were always a problem but it was not always easy to tell which of the drunks started the fight - especially if even the policeman was said to be drunk. A tale of fenland heavy drinking emerged from the Pear Tree beershop at Holbeach Marsh in October 1850. According to PC John Cain he went to the Pear Tree looking for someone, and ran into Thomas Wain whom he had arrested on a previous occasion. Wain apparently said, 'That's the b.... that locked me up, but I'll take care that he does not lock anyone else up.' Wain then drew a knife, but PC Cain went one better and drew a pistol. A sheepish Wain then sat down quietly but as PC Cain was leaving he was struck on the back of the head by a sharp instrument.

As can be expected, Thomas Wain told a very different story. He said that he had been drinking with PC Cain and two women and that the men had eleven pints between them. A drunken scuffle had then broken out during which the policeman had fallen among the pot mugs and cut his head. Witnesses provided a reason for the scuffle by saying that PC Cain had got the handcuffs out, waggled them in Wain's face and asked him if he'd like a night in gaol. The magistrates had the task of sorting out the truth and found Wain guilty of assault, being punished with two months' custody - not a severe punishment for assaulting a policeman, so they probably suspected the behaviour of PC Cain.

In December 1873 David Lee left the New Inn at Whaplode in a rowdy state and was told to be quiet by PC Tupps of Holbeach Bank. Lee made a charge at Tupps but the latter knocked him aside and into the dyke. Afterwards Tupps felt a pain in his arm and found that he had been stabbed. A knife was found in Lee's pocket and he was given two years' hard labour.

Another serious attack on a policeman occurred near Crowle on 8th February 1884. Two men were arrested but only one, Thomas Cunningham, was found guilty of shooting with intent to commit grievous bodily harm.

The incident occurred when a policeman was patrolling near Crowle and saw a gate to a field was open. When he went to the field he saw two men with guns and asked them their business. One of them, Cunningham, opened fire and the officer was shot behind the left ear. Cunningham then asked his companion, George Sharpe, for the other gun so he could fire again. The officer was able to run away, but was chased by Cunningham. The battered police helmet was produced as evidence in court. Cunningham was given seven years' penal servitude.

Arguments could also lead to violent assaults. In January 1874 two men were working in the stables at White Hall, Welbourn, when a dispute led to one stabbing the other in the thigh, a wound from which he nearly bled to death before help arrived. Such arguments could often be over very minor issues: John Sanderson of Grimsby was charged with assaulting Mrs Maria Hancock in a dispute over 'throwing water down a sink' but the case was dismissed.

Domestic disputes often ended in violence, but it was quite unusual for a servant to assault her mistress. This happened at Saxilby on 31st December 1861 when Mary Audas demanded her wages from her mistress, Mrs Dixon. The latter was relaxing in her sitting room when Audas entered and said she wanted to be paid as she could do no more work, but the servant was told to go away. The audacious servant replied by grabbing her mistress by the hair, whereupon Mrs Dixon screamed for help. Her daughter Catherine rushed in but was hit on the nose by the irate servant. Mrs Dixon brought a charge of assault against Mary Audas, who replied by bringing a similar charge against Catherine Dixon. Audas lost this legal battle and was fined £1 6s. plus costs.

An engaging picture of domestic disharmony in late-Victorian Lincoln was revealed when Henry Faulkner brought a charge of assault against Elizaman Lowe on 26th September 1893. Faulkner said that at 10.30pm that night his wife had left their house without permission and gone up the street. He went out after her and heard her voice at Mrs Lowe's house. However, Mrs Lowe chased him back down the street calling him unpleasant names and threatening to kill him; she was clearly a powerful and fierce woman.

Faulkner got back to his own house but Mrs Lowe caught him at the door and hit him in the chest. Her son then turned up and stopped her from continuing the assault, but promptly threatened to kill Faulkner himself.

In court Faulkner said that Mrs Lowe often abused him, at which the redoubtable woman could not contain her anger. 'It's a lie, you scamp,' she shouted, 'I never spoke to you, you lying villain,' thereby rather proving Faulkner's point. Faulkner said that Mrs Lowe had encouraged his wife to go to her house 'for improper purposes' and had pawned all his possessions and Mrs Faulkner had become 'Mrs Lowe's lodger.'

Mrs Lowe was fined 30s., which she refused to pay, so she went to prison instead. Faulkner asked for protection from her family, but the magistrates grew rather impatient and told him to move to another street.

There was certainly something strange going on in the relationship between William Cottingham and Mrs E. Todd, with the former having been bound over to keep the peace towards the latter. Despite this, in February 1844, Mrs Todd was found tied hand and foot to a tree in the park of Bayon's Manor near Tealby. It was believed that she had been 'left there to perish' though a claim that she was 'nearly starved to death' seems a little unlikely in that she had spent only three hours in close company with the tree. Cottingham was arrested and sentenced to three years in prison.

A highly unusual case of violence involved the 'Greetwell Duel' on 7th March 1874, all the more unusual in that the protagonists were fourteen and twelve years old respectively. Gerald Burn, the older, and George Seagrave were both boarders at the Pottergate Academy in Lincoln where they had been the best of friends until Gerald drew a caricature of George and stuck it up for everyone to laugh at. George tore it down, so Gerald challenged him to a duel.

The two schoolboys bought 'toy' pistols from a shop for 6*d*. each, but they seem to have been loaded with real gunpowder. All the pupils from the school went out to Greetwell fields to watch the duel, which was arranged in classic style with seconds. When it came to the time to fire, Seagrave's gun exploded in his hand, causing a bad wound, while Burn shot him in the leg with a bullet he had made himself.

Seagrave was in a bad state. 'I'm hit and losing blood fast,' he screamed, but he survived to tell the tale. Gerald Burn was arrested but found not guilty of any offence. The school does not come out of the event very well - it was reported that this was the second duel among its pupils, the first having been fought out by ten-year-olds!

Of course acts of petty violence were going on all the time, and many of them never reached the ears of the authorities. However, if a notable personality was involved then such events could make the headlines, and so it was that the Rector of Greetwell found his name splashed across the papers in 1877.

Rev. C. Ross was summonsed for assault on a Greetwell farmer's son, Campbell Neave, on 8th June 1877. Young Campbell was pasturing his sheep on the grass verge of one of the parish lanes as his father had bought the right to graze the land alongside each road. Ross, who lived nearby, said that the boy had no right to be there or to pasture his sheep on the verge, and further objected to them nibbling at his hedge. The boy challenged this, arguing that he had a perfect right to be there. The clergyman lost his temper, grabbed the boy by the collar, and pulled him off the road. In court, Ross admitted the assault and was fined 1*s*. with £1 2*s*. 6*d*. costs.

It was rare, however, for 'men of business' to settle their affairs by pitched battle, but exactly that happened in Boston in 1884. George Turner and George Housham were arrested for violating the Boston by-laws; they were fighting in Still Lane, which can hardly have lived up to its name that day. The arresting officer, PC Gilbert, found them with their clothes off and Turner bleeding from facial wounds.

593/12

THE
Crown Sentences,

FOR THE LINCOLNSHIRE SUMMER ASSIZES,

Holden at the Castle of Lincoln in and for the County of Lincoln, on Wednesday the Nineteenth day of July, 1848, before the Right Honorable Thomas Lord Denman, Chief Justice of our Lady the Queen assigned to hold Pleas before the Queen herself, and the Honorable Sir John Patterson, Knight; one other of the justices of our said Lady the Queen, also assigned to hold Pleas before the Queen herself.

Richard Ellison, Esq., Sheriff.

1. *William Mottashed*, aged 52, charged with having on the night of the 16th day of November, 1847, at Willoughby, in the parts of Lindsey, burglariously broken, and entered the dwelling house of Charles White with intent feloniously and burglariously to steal, take, and carry away the goods and chattels of the said Charles White. 7 *years transportation*.

2. *Joseph Travis*, aged 22, charged with having on the 19th day of December, 1847, at the parish of Kirton.

3. *William Fell*, 37, in the parts of Lindsey, feloniously, and violently stolen from the person of Charles Capeman, late of Blyborough, in the said parts, deceased, four pieces of the current gold coin, of this realm, called sovereigns, of the value of fourpounds, two pieces of the current silver coin of this realm, called half crowns of the value of five shillings, two shillings, one sixpence, one bunch of keys, one pocket knife, and various other articles the property of the said Charles Capeman, deceased. Fell admitted evidence, Travis transported for life.

4. *Maria Cliffe*, 21, charged for that she on the 28th day of February, 1848, at Gainsborough in the parts of Lindsey, feloniously and unlawfully did attempt to strangle her female bastard child, with intent then and there feloniously, wilfully, and of her malice aforethought, her female bastard child to kill and murder against the form of the statute in that case made and provided. 12 *months imprisonment*.

5. *Thomas Johnson*, aged 26 charged with having on the 18th day of April, 1848, at Metheringham, in the parts of Kesteven, did unlawfully, unjustly, and deceitfully utter to one Peter Grantham, and Edward Woodhouse, one false and counterfeit coin called sixpence, well knowing the same to be false and counterfeit. 9 *months & 2 days*.

6. *William Harley*, aged 24, charged with having on the 18th day of April, 1848, at Potterhanworth in the parts of Kesteven, did unlawfully, unjustly, and deceitfully utter to one Thomas Linton, one piece of false and counterfeit coin called a sixpence, and on the same day at Metheringham, in the said parts, one other piece of false and counterfeit coin, did unlawfully, unjustly, and deceitfully utter to one John Scholey, well knowing the same to be counterfeit. 1 *year & 1 days imprisonment*.

7. *Ann Smith*, aged 18, charged with having on the 3rd day of May, 1848, at Bourn, in the parts of Kesteven feloniously, wilfully, and maliciously set fire to a wheat stack, the property of Joseph Smith. 18 *months imp*.

8. *Philip Lowe*, aged 30, charged with having on the 23rd day of August, 1846, at Beverley, in the County of York, feloniously,& unlawfully married one Mary Thornton, Ann Lowe his former wife being alive. 1 *years imp*.

9. *William Burdett*, aged 33, charged with having on the 27th day of September, 1847, at the parish of Holy Trinity, in the Town of Kingston upon Hull, feloniously, and unlawfully married one Ann Bird, Ann Burdett his former wife being then alive. 9 *calendar months imprisonment*.

10. *Thomas Austin*, aged 26, charged with having on the night of the 20th day of June, 1848, at the Township of Glamford Briggs, in the parts of Lindsey, feloniously, and burglariously broken and entered the dwelling house of Thomas Dawson, and feloniously steal therefrom a watch of the value of twenty shillings, a watch key of the value of one penny, and fourteen cigars of the value of two shillings, of the goods and chattels of the said Thomas Dawson 1 *years imprisonment*.

11. *Thomas Clow*, aged 22, charged with feloniously and carnally knowing and abusing Catherine Gilroy, on the 28th of June, 1848, at Cowbit in the parts of Holland gainst the statue in such case made and provided. 1 *years imp*.

12. *George Beales*, aged 21, charged for that they on the night of the 1st, of July 1848, at Spalding in the Parts.

13. *William Veal*, 21, of Holland burglariously broken and entered the dwelling house of Edward Thompson, and feloniously steal therefrom one silver watch of value of one Pound the property of James Harlick, of Spalding, also one Knife of the value of Sixpence the property of Edward Whyman, of Spalding. *Beales 10 & Veal 7years transportation*.

14. *Elizabeth Garner*, aged 13 charged on suspicion with having at Calceby, in the parts of Lindsey, feloniously administered or attempted to administer to one Mary Smith, with intent then and there feloniously, wilfully, & of her malice aforethought, the said Mary Smith, to poison, kill, and murder, against the form of the statute in such case made and provided. *death recorded*.

15. *James Hingley*, charged with breaking into the counting house of H. Smith, and others on the 15th of July at Gainsboro' and stealing therefrom divers monies the property of the said H. Smith & others. 10 *years transportation*.

Prisoner in the City Gaol.

15. *Thomas Wightman*, aged 32, Sawyer, charged with having on the 29th, of May last in the parish of St. Mary-le-Wigtord feloniously stabbed one James Goodlad, with intent to murder, maim, disfigure, disable or him some grievous bodily harm. *Not Guilty*.

B. E. LEARY, PRINTER & BOOKBINDER, 19, STRAIT, LINCOLN.

The Crown Sentences of Sheriff Richard Ellison, 1848
Lincolnshire Archives

In court Housham, a corn merchant, said that Turner — a rival — had annoyed him when doing business by pushing up against him and treading on his toes. They were each fined £1.

Tradesmen also got into disputes with each other about money. At the Sleaford sessions in July 1895 butcher John Brown of Ruskington charged the Dorrington carrier, John Reynolds, with assaulting him at Sleaford on 10th June. There was also a 'cross-summons' of Brown by Reynolds.

The dispute arose because Brown owed some money to Reynolds, but refused to pay it until the latter had paid his own account for meat supplied. After a too-lengthy visit to the Carre Arms in Sleaford, the two got into a dispute which came to blows when Reynolds — an elderly man — hit Brown on the nose. The court fined Reynolds 5s. and Brown 2s. 6d., but it was the former who 'was cheered on going down the steps.'

Finally, a mention should be made of people who used the threat of violence to obtain money. This sort of offence was very rare but it did occur in 1892 when Charles Kershaw tried to get money from two Lindsey magistrates by threatening to kill them. Charles Kershaw had worked at Marshall & Co.'s Gainsborough ironworks until a brief period in prison, after which James Marshall refused to re-employ him despite letters from a charitable organisation. Kershaw therefore bore a grudge against Marshall, a Lindsey magistrate, and sent a letter threatening to kill him unless £5 was paid over. The small sum of money stipulated emphasises the amateurishness of this scheme. Kershaw also demanded £10 from another Lindsey magistrate, Francis Gamble.

The letters were easily traced and Kershaw was arrested at Hyde in Cheshire on 18th October 1892. He pleaded guilty in the Marshall case and was sentenced to two months' hard labour, the fairly light sentence reflecting the rather pathetic nature of this case.

CHAPTER THREE: THIEVES AND ROBBERS

In the early Victorian period crimes against property, such as theft, were regarded as being just as serious as — if not more so than — crimes of violence. Punishments could be harsh, as can be seen from the two months in prison given to John Matthews of Brigg in 1854 for stealing a smock; but in 1844 William Springthorpe and John Fish were transported for life after offences that would be considered minor today: the former stole a watch and £5, the latter a single sheep. The same year James Gaven stole two live rabbits from Charles Pirotte of Horncastle, for which he was sentenced to four years' penal servitude.

Most minor robberies were dealt with by the magistrates or at the Quarter Sessions. A survey of the Lincoln City Quarter Sessions at the beginning of the era shows the variety of offences likely to be committed. Labourer Richard Usher was charged with theft from William Chapman in January 1838; his 'booty' included a pair of earrings (worth 8s.), three brooches (15s.), one ring (5s.), one pin (1s.), a silver thimble (1s. 6d.) and a metal thimble (6d.). This princely haul cost him six months in the House of Correction, including three weeks in 'solitary.'

The Quarter Sessions records show that punishments escalated rapidly for property crimes. At the Lincoln City Quarter Sessions of July 1838 Spencer Wallhead received one week's hard labour for stealing a silver teaspoon but John Scoley got four months' hard labour after pleading guilty to the theft of a handkerchief. William Davis, who stole about £5 worth of property from Mary Squire, was transported for fifteen years! At the opposite end of the scale, Caroline West stole a spoon worth 1s. 6d. and had to spend half an hour in the House of Correction.

It is easy to see how young people drifted into crime in Victorian days just as they may be tempted to do today. Mary Atkinson and Eleanor Kelly were both girls of about 17 years old and living in Bourne in 1851, when they began a slide into criminal habits. Mary Atkinson was the daughter-in-law of Christopher Peck, and they preyed upon this man by getting the keys to his house and stealing a shilling, two sovereigns and two handkerchiefs. Atkinson got 16 days in Folkingham gaol and Kelly 14 days.

Perhaps more surprising was that established citizens with a lot to lose also yielded to such temptations. In October 1846 William Graham, a house surgeon at Lincoln Asylum (now The Lawn Centre), was sentenced to four months' hard labour for stealing a gold watch from a patient. Of course the ruin of his career was a life sentence. More peculiar still was the behaviour of a dentist from Salford who was visiting Lincoln in 1877: he stole some forceps from another dentist! This offence cost him nine months' hard labour.

At a more dangerous level were the vicious thieves and 'footpads' who haunted dark streets at night, waiting for helpless passers-by to ambush. These often worked in gangs and were armed with a variety of weapons, such as the 'life-preserver' or a strip of canvas filled with sand. A method that received special publicity was the garotte, whereby the victim was disabled through crushing pressure on his throat. In April 1853 Thomas Winn was going through his garden gate at Newland in Lincoln when he was assaulted in this way by three men, who stole five £10 notes and a purse containing £8. However, they were captured and despatched to the colonies for 15 years.

To the Victorians, the most terrifying type of robber was the one that broke into your house, especially if he brought a gang of accomplices with him. In December 1855 the house of elderly James Pooles at Sutterton was attacked by two men with blackened faces, who attempted to force their way in through the door. Pooles got out of bed but the men broke in and struck him on the head with an iron bar before stealing 19s. 2d. They were believed to be local men as it was known that Pooles had sold a large quantity of wheat, but in fact he had not kept this money in his house. The men were never caught.

A common trick was to burgle the house of someone who had been seen going to church, since the criminals could be sure they would be away for a set amount of time. John Wass and William York broke into the house of Rebecca Rowett at Stixwould on 2nd February 1868. She had gone to church at 5pm and returned to find the door open. Two half-crowns, a gold ring, a pair of spectacles and a razor were missing. Two men had been seen loitering near the house by a shoemaker and they were traced to Bardney, where they had used the money to get lodgings. They were arrested there and received eight months' hard labour.

Early in 1868 a Miss Whitwell of Holbeach Road, Spalding, was asleep in bed at 2.15am when she was suddenly woken by a heavy blow to her body. Terrified, she leapt out of bed but was grabbed by the throat by one of two burglars. 'Hear me, blessed heavenly Father,' she shrieked, and the men ran off. Whether by divine intervention or not, their hasty departure surprised a policeman who was walking along the road and they were arrested. John Brooks and Nathaniel Smith were given a year of hard labour apiece. One of them had been a tenant in a house of Miss Whitwell's.

Some burglars seem to have been easily satisfied with what they could steal quickly. John Wilcox stole only a calico sheet from a house at Kirton near Boston in July 1862 and the following day stole only a few clothes from a house in Algarkirk. His punishment of four years' penal servitude must have felt out of all proportion to the crime.

In 1877 two men burgled the house of Edward Woodhouse at Kirton-in-Lindsey, for which they were sentenced to hard labour of six and nine months' duration. Their 'haul' was a typical motley collection: a coat, a waistcoat, a brooch, two silk handkerchiefs, a jacket, a pair of drawers and a shirt. The same year a Long Sutton burglar received a year's hard labour for stealing two pairs of boots, a pair of spectacles, a candle and a teaspoon!

Burglars could generally be divided into cases of habitual criminals and those who succumbed to a sudden temptation. Among the latter were two teenagers from Bardney: James Caborn and James Horton, aged 17 and 15 respectively. They worked for a farmer who kept a stack in the yard of a house belonging to Fanny Pinning. Miss Pinning went off to Spilsby and closed her house up, but the temptation was too strong for the two lads who broke in and stole four bottles of wine and a mirror. The broken window was noticed by a neighbour and, when two of the missing bottles were found in the nearby stack, little detection was needed to find the culprits. They each received six weeks' hard labour in April 1884.

A lot of petty theft involved something that could be eaten. George Watson stole two ducks, worth 6s., at Grantham on 25th February 1866. He was stopped at 7.30am on a Sunday morning by a policeman, who wanted to know what was in his basket, there being no trade on a Sunday. The basket proved to contain duck feathers and entrails, connecting Watson to the news of two missing ducks. Indeed the rest of the ducks were found beneath the floorboards of his house and his bootmarks were discovered at the scene of the crime. He received six months' hard labour.

A rather miserable case in December 1841 involved William Neal, a farmworker from Holbeach. He worked for William Welch, who became suspicious when he heard that Neal had sold some potatoes to a local shoemaker. It says a lot for the standard of living of the time that Welch knew Neal did not have any potatoes, and he soon found some footmarks leading from his own potato pile to Neal's house. Neal was given three months' hard labour. In contrast, two Spalding schoolboys who stole four chocolate sweets worth 2*d.* in 1884 received three strokes of the birch each.

The publican at Lincoln's Ripon Arms seems to have been interested in stealing food and garden produce in general. George Brailsford stole asparagus and rhubarb from a chimney-sweep's garden on a regular basis. Eventually the sweep decided to hide in his privy in the middle of the garden and caught Brailsford climbing over the fence. Brailsford was found to have also stolen geraniums from a market gardener. In mitigation he was said to be an alcoholic. He was fined £5. Perhaps the most interesting aspect of this case is that Victorian sweeps ate asparagus (or hoped to).

Richard Poole broke into the shop of Myra Curtois at Saxilby on 21st May 1895. He stole ham, bread, buns and sugar, then took them all home. Sergeant Holmes was soon on his trail and knocked loudly on Poole's door, but the thief said he could not let the officer in as he had no clothes on. Sergeant Holmes waited quietly until he smelt something burning, whereupon he called in at the blacksmith's to get a key. He let himself into Poole's house, but the latter tried to keep him at bay with a hay fork. However, the bread burning in the fireplace gave the game away and Poole received two month hard labour.

Some types of food were easier to steal than others, and food that could walk along by itself had special attractions. The stealing of sheep is dealt with in chapter six, but we should mention here the theft of cattle. Sometimes this was very simple, as with two men who simply led off a cow from Lincoln's West Common in July 1847. Unfortunately for them, their tracks were followed to Dunholme and they were given four months in prison.

Another 'food thief' received only rough justice at Burton near Lincoln in September 1841. This was a local rogue who stole farm labourers' dinners while they were working at the harvest. When they suspected what was happening the men set a trap and when they had caught the thief they trussed him up and put him in a sack, tying it tight around his neck. One of them drew a large pocket knife and gave the villain a very rough shave, without soap or water. 'The poor fellow's cries were most miserable,' it was reported.

In 1893 a gang of men operated by stealing birds and animals in the Frithville district, their speciality being ducks. Six were stolen from Joseph Bowser of Frithville and were found in a pond belonging to Ben Booth, the gang's ringleader, still with their markings. The gang had stolen twenty ducks from another man in Frithville and seventeen from Sibsey.

Occasionally people even tried to steal from a church. At Long Sutton in 1874 two sixteen-year-old boys broke into the Baptist chapel and stole 30s. They were given fourteen days in prison and ten strokes of the birch.

If a robbery had taken place, strangers were always likely to come under suspicion, especially if they were gypsies or pedlars. On 25th June 1866 Mrs Jane Moffat was tending her public house in Dunholme when the tax collector arrived, followed quickly by a hawker named Thomas Gorman. Mrs Moffat paid the tax man £8 and 3d. for cattle plague rates and poor rates, but left her purse in the tap room. When she returned it had gone and, as Gorman was the only customer she had seen, she presumed he was the thief. In fact Gorman had left Dunholme by the 'foot road' to Ryland and Wickenby station and was not arrested until three days later. Meanwhile Dunholme carpenter John Doubikin had found the purse, and some money, in the grass along Ryland lane. Gorman, though, was shown to be of previous good character and with little solid evidence against him the case was dismissed.

Clever thieves even managed to disguise their activities with an element of the confidence trick. In 1840 a farm servant of Rev. P. Curtois at Branston, Cammack, sold some of his master's sheep for £45 and unwisely called in at the Wheat Sheaf on the way home. There he met a man who said he owed Mr Curtois a sovereign. He pressed the coin upon Cammack and also gave him a letter to pass to his employer. The man was so concerned about the safe delivery of the letter that Cammack was wholly convinced, so imagine his dismay when he got home to find the £45 missing and the 'letter' a simple piece of blank paper. Cammack's disgust (not to say Mr Curtois') must have been complete when he found that the sovereign was a fake.

A common criminal tactic was to prey on people disabled by alcohol, a practice known as bug-hunting. One bug who was caught this way was elderly John Gringham who came to Lincoln with money in two bags. He went to the Cross Keys public house and got involved in a discussion with William Harding, in which he boasted of his wealth. Cannily, Harding bet the old man a glass of ale that he could not show him a sovereign, so Gringham got his money bag out, produced the sovereign and drank some more beer. Foolishly he left the bag on the table and an hour or two later Harding grabbed it and ran off, Gringham not being in any sort of state to chase him. However, Harding was well-known and soon brought into custody, receiving two years' hard labour.

The combination of a man with money, plenty of drink and a 'loose woman' was even more likely to end in tears. In July 1855 a Washingborough wheelwright, Benjamin Woodhead, was enjoying the dubious pleasures of a night-out in Lincoln. Having already consumed a formidable amount of drink, he was tempted by the doubtful attractions of Mrs Harriet Tester, 'a notorious prostitute.' Mrs Tester enticed him down Much Lane to Harrison's dram shop, a shoddy establishment which maintained a 'room at the back' where women such as Mrs Tester could entertain their clients. Mrs Tester, though, took the opportunity to relieve Woodhead of his purse and, when challenged, she was seen to drop it. She was punished with a year's hard labour, but Woodhead also received his punishment with his name being published in the papers - no doubt to the delight of all the other Washingborough villagers.

Crowds provided useful cover for the pickpocket. Lincoln Fair was notorious for thieves, but still attracted foolish men and women with valuables in their pockets. Lincoln solicitor Alexander Trotter went to the fair in April 1893 and was relieved of a watch and silver match-box by Edward Boyne. This man was clearly a semi- professional thief operating in a wide area, since he tried to sell the match-box to a Leeds jeweller, who was suspicious as the initials had been crudely scratched off. Lincoln jeweller James Usher identified it as one he had sold to Trotter and so Boyne went to prison for nine months.

Grimsby market was another attractive place for criminals. In July 1868 a young woman lost her purse, containing 4s. 6d., which she reported to Sergeant Allbones. He watched the crowds carefully and was soon able to arrest Henry Fielding (presumably no relation to the author and creator of the Bow Street Runners) and John Watson. The two villains had long coats with the bottoms cut out of the pockets, so they could pick other people's pockets while appearing to have their hands in their own.

Pickpockets were among the most persistent of the habitual criminals. In January 1884 Sarah Hobson was walking along Lincoln High Street when she had to find her way through a group of men standing around on High Bridge. As she went by she felt a hand move along her pocket, and discovered her purse, containing £1 7s. 6d., had been taken. She had her suspicions as to who had it and spoke to the man directly, and he promptly confirmed her suspicions by running away down some steps.

Had the pickpocket known Lincoln he would have realised that his 'escape route' was a cul-de-sac. When sentencing him to five years' penal servitude, the judge noted he had convictions in Lincoln, Nottingham, Chester, Birkdale, Newcastle, Rugby, Warwick and Wolverhampton.

Any idea that shoplifting is a modern practice is soon dispelled through a study of Victorian events, although shoplifters of that period had greater difficulty as fewer goods were kept on open display. On 27th December 1854 Robert Sewards attempted to steal 1*lb* of mixed coffee from a shop at Corby Glen. He used the old trick of buying several other things as a cover, in this case his main purchase being ½*lb* of butter for 7*d*. Shopkeeper Mr Willerton 'observed something mysterious in his movements' and Sewards was arrested at home where the missing coffee was discovered. He claimed that 'a lad had purchased it for him,' but no lad could be produced. He was given a month's hard labour.

Even less subtle were four 'gipsy tribe' characters who were being watched by a suspicious policeman in Grantham's Watergate in February 1874. At 9.30pm on a Saturday night they bought a small piece of mutton from a butcher's shop, but the policeman saw Eliza Smith 'wrap something up in a cloth.' Each of the 'gipsies' got a month's hard labour.

Because many of the wealthier Lincolnshire citizens employed servants, there was a constant procession through the courts of people who had succumbed to the temptation to pilfer goods from their employers. Emma Tutty, aged sixteen, worked for Mr and Mrs Alford at Friskney in 1874 and it would seem that the Alfords became suspicious of her. They arranged to 'go out' for the evening leaving Tutty and a lad behind, but two policeman watched the house. A light flashed from an upstairs window and then the lad was sent out to 'watch the road' while Jonathan Miller (aged eighteen) used a knife to break in through the sitting room window. Emma Tutty then handed out wine, cakes and cigars through the window, at which point the constables pounced. This very childish attempt to fake a burglary as an excuse for the missing objects cost Miller and Tutty six months in prison each.

Sarah Marsh, a seventeen-year-old servant at Snarford, stole the clothes of her own mistress, Mary Allen, in 1874. The things that disappeared included three lady's jackets, a silk sash and two white dresses. Marsh was given 15 months' hard labour.

Tetford housekeeper Mary Pickford clearly nursed a grudge against her employer, which she satisfied when leaving the job at the age of 62.

She took the opportunity to remove a silver cream jug and six forks, a crime as stupid as it was pointless. She received one month in prison.

Servant girls were notoriously prey to suitors with an eye on the house where they worked. A victim of this proved to be the impressionable Mary Townsend, who worked for Charles Titley, landlord of the Marquis of Granby in Louth. George Smith persuaded Townsend that he wanted to marry her, then outlined a plan where she should pilfer as much as she could from the inn, then get herself dismissed so that they could run off together without seeming suspicious. Smith had already been in prison, but told Townsend that he needed the money for new clothes. Townsend had pilfered 30s. before she was caught, whereupon Smith disappeared. The court dismissed the charges against the girl, who had clearly been easily deceived.

Some robberies were the work of elaborately organised gangs and these often involved more notable local figures such as tradesmen. One such group was operating a wool-stealing racket around Glentworth in 1851. About 400 fleeces were stolen from Mr Hood of Nettleham and others from Atkinson of Fillingham and Clarke of Glentworth. The wool was hidden on the premises of Barnard, who operated the Glentworth carrier's service and thus had perfect cover for his illicit activities, which included moving the stolen wool for sale in Lincoln and Gainsborough.

Eventually the gang was arrested and men from Gainsborough, Glentworth, Hemswell and Nettleham were charged with stealing 144*lbs*. of wool at West Firsby. Wool was found hidden under a pile of dung and straw on Barnard's premises and in a large storage pit concealed beneath a heap of coal behind a house in Gainsborough. George Barnard, the apparent ringleader, was given two years' hard labour.

CHAPTER FOUR:
HIGHWAYS, RAILWAYS & WATERWAYS

1. Crimes of the Lanes & Highways

The Victorian Age was not the golden period of the highwayman; for that had been fifty or sixty years before Victoria ascended the throne. However, this did not mean that road travel was safe, for the roads and byways were still the haunt of many desperate characters. There was, though, a notable change of style and victim.

The 'classic' highwayman preyed on the rich by holding up stagecoaches. By Victorian times the typical highway criminal was an uncultured and brutal thug looking for an easy chance, which meant that victims were generally poorer people who could not claim the safety of horseback. It also meant that any drunk was especially liable to be attacked.

It was unusual for men on foot to attack another on horseback, but of course those who could afford a horse were more likely to be worth robbing. In April 1839 a Mr Ward was riding from Washingborough to Waddington when he was attacked by four men near Red Hall. One of the men seized the reins of the horse, whereupon Ward produced a pistol and fired. Unfortunately for Ward, his gun misfired and the men gave him a violent beating. They stole nine sovereigns and 7s. 6d. in coins before running off 'towards Sleaford', which was a long way from the scene of the crime on foot, but apparently a town that was thought to be a den of thieves.

A case that probably brought its perpetrators great popularity with ordinary folk occurred on 12th September 1838. The victim, Peter Johnson, was Master of the Gainsborough workhouse and thus likely to be a detested figure among the ranks of the poor. He was attacked at 10.45pm by two young men named Birch and Hudson, who held him down and went through his pockets. In March 1839 they were sentenced to fifteen years' penal servitude.

Some victims of highway crime were foolish in the extreme. One who should have known better was William North, the Carlton Scroop schoolmaster. In January 1855 he travelled from Lincoln to Sleaford by horse bus and then made a tour of the town's dubious hostelries. In one of these he met 'Berry Houghton,' a dissolute and unreliable young man. The more North drank, the more he sought to impress his new friend by boasting of his wealth, although other more responsible citizens in the public house warned him to be quiet.

By 9.30pm North was fairly merry and agreed to let Houghton accompany him home in return for a half sovereign and a good supper. The schoolmaster was too drunk to know much about what was happening, so Houghton led him off towards Silk Willoughby, south rather than west. Near the village Houghton did the inevitable deed; he knocked North into the ditch, stealing a £5 note and £4 10s. in gold. Houghton then ran off but North got back on his feet and trudged back to Sleaford, no doubt sobered up by his experience and the cold January night. The police were called and raided Houghton's house, where they found the villain sitting beside the fire with North's money still in his pockets. There was quite a fight before they managed to arrest him. It is hard to say who was the more foolish: the drunken schoolmaster or the simplistic villain.

In November 1855 a cottager from Ingoldmells named Brown was returning home from chapel at night when he was set upon by three men with blackened faces. This was also a typical form of attack, for groups of men could rob a victim more efficiently and securely than a man on his own. They tripped Brown up, searched through his pockets and ran off, but without the £15 he had hidden on him.

Another who had cause to rue a visit to a hostelry was Irishman Martin Roughlican. The Irishman had come to Lincolnshire in 1873 to help with the harvest but had stayed on at Cabourn near Caistor. On 4th October he walked to Caistor in order to get a £7 postal order to send to his mother and while there he had a drink at the 'Red Lion' with a few other men from the farm. Roughlican's friends left but he stayed on to buy a drink for an old man before hurrying on behind them. However, Roughlican's time in the pub had clearly tempted him to talk about the money he was sending back to Ireland and while he was still alone a man leapt out of a dyke beside the road and pulled him over while a second kicked him in the face. The two men stole Roughlican's purse, containing 16s. 8d., and the £7 postal order. However, he knew both men and they were soon caught and given 14 months in prison.

A rare case of a man declaring himself to be a highwayman took place on 30th May 1844. Jacob Gainsley was the pious keeper of the Kenwick Thorn toll-bar at Tathwell near Louth. At about 8pm he was sitting in the tollgate cottage reading his Bible with his wife beside him and his son upstairs when William Markham came in and asked for some ginger beer.

Markham asked Gainsley about his Bible and the tollkeeper told him that he had just bought it for 1s. 9d. which was a blessing compared to the prices people had had to pay in past generations. Markham walked over to a brace of pistols which were kept near the mantle-shelf and calmly said, 'You don't know I'm a highwayman.' He then fired at Jacob Gainsley's head, but missed.

The Gainsleys' son rushed down at the sound of the gun and grappled with Markham who shot him in the arm. Jacob Gainsley managed to stab Markham with a swordstick, but the highwayman then drew out a cut-throat razor and threatened to kill himself. The elder Gainsley was quite shocked at this suggestion and pleaded with Markham not to do it, but Markham used the razor to cut the son's hand before running off.

A search for the highwayman was made and he was arrested at a house in Bilsby where he actually did try to kill himself with the razor. Dr Handsley of Alford sewed the wound up, but no sooner had he finished the job than Markham tore it open again. The desperate highwayman was sentenced to life transportation.

Robberies were not the only offences to be committed that involved roads. Victorian Lincolnshire had its own 'traffic offences,' some of which seem quite prosaic compared to driving offences today. 'Dangerous driving' certainly did exist as can be seen from what happened to William Weselby of Dorrington, who was prosecuted at the instigation of the owner of the Lincoln to Sleaford omnibus in January 1855. Weselby's offences included riding on the shafts of the wagon, galloping with a wagon and obstructing the highway. He was fined one shilling.

Another common 'dangerous driving' offence was driving or riding on a team of horses without reins, which seems to have been one way in which Lincolnshire youth expressed their machismo in the 1800s. George Richardson of Gayton-le-Wold was fined a hefty 17s. for doing this on a turnpike in 1855. The authorities seem to have made periodic attempts to stamp out what was clearly a rural form of 'macho' behaviour; in February 1877 several people were fined 8s. or 9s. at Louth and a waggoner at North Cockerington was fined 8s. as well.

Other traffic offences included not being in proper control of a horse and cart. The Withern hawker, Charles Atkin, was fined for being too far from his cart on the road at Authorpe; typically, this offence brought in people who let the horse carry on with the cart while they lagged behind to pick blackberries or talk to cottagers.

Some vehicles had to be licensed. In 1865 John Rylatt of Potter-hanworth was prosecuted for keeping a 'stage carriage' at Branston without a license. He was fined £5 for each of three offences.

For much of the period road maintenance was the responsibility of each parish, for which task a sometimes-reluctant 'Surveyor of Highways' was supposed to be in charge. Of course everything focussed on how to spend as little as possible and do as little as possible without falling foul of the law. In February 1874 the Metheringham surveyor, Elvidge, was summonsed for allowing the roads to get out of repair. A policeman had complained frequently to him, but Elvidge 'pooh-poohed' his comments. The road between Metheringham and Dunston was especially bad and no stone was prepared for it. However, once the summons was taken out there was a sudden start on its repair, but too late for Elvidge to escape a fine of £1.

A Lincolnshire country lane, giving an excellent idea of the conditions faced by travellers in the Victorian age.

Parishes were especially reluctant to repair 'main' roads that were of little use to local traffic. Also in 1874, the surveyors of West Firsby, Fillingham and Saxby were prosecuted for allowing 'Hermin-street' to degenerate. An 800 yard section had ruts ten inches deep while in other parts stones had been put down that were too big and these had injured horses. The parish surveyors were each fined £1 with 12s. costs.

Not everyone respected the majesty of the Queen's highways. In January 1855 William Clarke of Market Rasen was fined 11s. for blocking Willingham Road with 'a large heap of manure.' In July 1893 Charles Jacklin of Theddlethorpe was fined 5s. for 'depasturing the highway' with five beasts, an offence which seems to conjure up the truly rural nature of life in Victorian Lincolnshire!

2. Railway Crimes

In the Victorian period it was relatively common for railway employees to be charged with manslaughter following fatal accidents to passengers or other railway workers. Accidents occurred regularly, for the basic mechanical methods of controlling trains and signals had few fail-safe functions. It was, however, very difficult to get a jury to convict a railway worker on a manslaughter charge.

Some manslaughter cases were brought rather unnecessarily. On 10th January 1874 there was a collision at Barkston Junction (then spelt 'Barkstone') north of Grantham, in which Henry Crawford and Arthur Casburn lost their lives. At Barkston, the line from Scotland to King's Cross was joined by the branch-line from Boston and Sleaford. The night of the accident was very foggy and the driver of the 6pm from Boston, John Whittle, failed to stop at the danger signals.

Although the Barkston signalman waved frantically with a hand-lamp, Whittle's train ran through the warnings and collided with an 'up' Scotch 3rd class train. The engine of the Scottish train was badly damaged and its fireman, Arthur Casburn, was scalded to death. The damaged train was hit by a northbound cattle train and the second body, Crawford's, was found beneath the wreckage. Whittle was arrested and charged with manslaughter on the assumption that his carelessness had caused the two deaths; the case against him was dismissed when it was proved that the conditions on the night made it very difficult for a driver to locate his position or see the signals in time.

Some railway workers did go to prison for their carelessness. In 1865 Edward Jackson, signalman in the parish of Branston on the Boston to

Lincoln line, was given one month hard labour for endangering lives by his failure to show a green flag.

There were others whose behaviour could have caused an accident and these would nowadays be labelled as 'vandals.' One such was Enoch Wilson, who got drunk on 9th June 1866 and moved a signal lever from danger to clear at the Durham Ox signalbox of the Great Northern Railway in Lincoln. When confronted by the signalman, Wilson said, 'I hope you will forgive me.' The court was very lenient in simply binding him over.

More traditional vandalism was perpetrated by William Barnsdale on the Great Northern line near Swineshead when he twice placed objects on the line to see what would happen. On 12th September 1892 he put a piece of iron on the track and nine days later put a chunk of wood in the same place. He was given three months' hard labour.

A more imaginative example of potentially destructive behaviour occurred on the Midland Railway's Lincoln branch in 1848. Three porters from the Midland station at Lincoln and three of their friends decided to borrow a 'manumotive' belonging to the railway contractors, Peto & Betts. Using their own muscle power, the young men set off for a Sunday outing to Newark. They spent the afternoon at the Nottinghamshire market town and, inevitably, returned to the manumotive in a fairly tipsy condition. Nonetheless they set off for home but only got as far as Collingham before they had to abandon their motive power and walk the rest of the way. All six were arrested and the sentences, including hard labour, varied from five weeks to two weeks in gaol.

Of course there were occasional disturbances actually on the trains, generally involving the consumption of alcohol. In March 1866 Mr Goose, a farmer from Branston Fen, was summonsed by a Mr Cox for assault after a fight in a train on the short journey from Lincoln to Washingborough. Ironically Goose was fined though he had come out the worse in the fight.

The transport of goods by rail allowed many opportunities for criminal conduct, but not always by straightforward robbers. For example, John Robinson of Langworth attempted to defraud the Manchester, Sheffield & Lincolnshire Railway when sending some timber to Lincoln. He gave a false estimate of the size of timber, thereby saving himself 11s. 3d. on the freight charge. The court fined him £3 5s. 0d.

There were many occasions on which goods were simply stolen from railway stations. In January 1857 three men stole twenty stones of flour, twelve stones of candles and a box from the MSLR at Market Rasen. They were easily caught, one having hid the wheat at his father's house.

Guards on trains were expected to be of exemplary character and in some companies had to have friends to put forward a bond against their good behaviour. The reason for this can be seen from the behaviour of Joseph Laverack, a Great Northern guard. He was in charge of a train on the East Lincolnshire line on 12th July 1851 and one of the items in a van was a cask of tobacco being sent from Leeds to Alford. When the train reached Sibsey, Laverack transferred the cask from its van to his own luggage compartment. However, the cask clearly did not yield easily to his depredations, since when the train stopped at Old Leake he borrowed a hammer and chisel from the engine driver.

When the tobacco cask was checked at Alford it was found to be 'light' in its weight, whereupon chisel marks were also discovered. Laverack's house was searched and 8½*lbs* of tobacco were found. He was given a year in prison.

In January 1855 Grantham magistrates censured the Great Northern Railway for being careless with its own property. This followed the arrest in 1854 of William Marston, for stealing 28*lb* of rail at Spittlegate in the town. Marston spent three months in custody before his case came up so the GNR did not press charges, but the magistrates awarded him 14 days in any case and complained that the Great Northern should not leave its property lying about.

Railways were huge businesses which collected money in many different ways, so they were always at risk of being defrauded. This was not always helped by their loose accounting practices. Money from Boston goods depot was sent in a bag to the house of William Dixon, the booking clerk, at West Street toll bar. The money was first counted by the goods staff and then meant to be checked by Dixon.

On 29th November 1854 a leather bag containing £60 6s. 3d. was sent to Dixon's house, arriving at 7.50pm. Dixon did not check it until the next day, when he found 19s. 6d. missing. The missing money was soon traced to Dixon's 14-year-old servant, Elizabeth Beecham, who had just bought a silk bonnet for 19s. 6d. Boston magistrates gave the girl three months in prison, but they also complained about the loose practices of the Great Northern, especially the fact that the leather money bag was not locked away.

Honest, tee-total 'Navvies' at lunch, from a contemporary temperance anthology.

One of the most protracted legal cases saw a railway company in court. This involved the alleged nuisance caused by the Great Northern Railway's level crossing over Lincoln High Street. There had been regular battles between the GNR and Lincoln since the station was first opened, but these had appeared to be resolved by a ruling from the Board of Trade in 1868 which banned the GNR from 'shunting' over the crossing.

Of course this ruling called into question what the exact legal definition of shunting actually was. The GNR and the Urban Sanitary Authority (a part of the Corporation) had different definitions, and so in February 1877 the latter tried to prosecute the former in the Lincoln Police Court for alleged 'nuisance' as the Public Health Act allowed a fine of 40s. for obstructing a highway. The Corporation employed an ex-GNR man to watch the crossing at High Street and also the Pelham Street one, recording any 'shunting' that obstructed the highway. As a result 21 summonses were issued against the GNR, sixteen of them being for High Street.

The 'watchman' had been on duty on 5th January 1877 when, it was alleged, the High Street had been blocked by 'shunting' from 11.05am to 11.06am. This had inconvenienced 21 people and two vehicles. An interesting discussion then ensued as to what was 'shunting,' the train in question having been a short working of a couple of laden wagons from the station to the Holmes goods depot. The magistrates ruled that if such a train was illegal, then the GNR would not be able to operate its railway at all; the case was dismissed, as was a second one when Pelham Street crossing was blocked by some empty carriages for a Louth train being brought into the station. Following this all the other cases were dropped and the ratepayers were presumably out of pocket, and still inconvenienced.

The GNR was in trouble on another occasion when it had to stir the corporate coffers to pay a fine of £3. In February 1884 it transported three calves, under a month old, from Boston to Hubbert's Bridge without a licence to show that the animals were free of contagious diseases. Both the GNR and the recipient, farmer James Bowles of Algarkirk Fen, were fined.

3. River & Coast

The long and remote coast of Lincolnshire made it a natural attraction for smugglers, but the Victorian period was not the golden age of smuggling since the fashion for 'free trade' had reduced a lot of import duties, making smuggling less attractive. Smuggling was mostly a part-time activity for people who used their boats for other legitimate activities. However, the many boats and ships that plied the rivers and coast of Lincolnshire generated a surprisingly diverse criminal world of their own.

The main trade for Lincolnshire's smugglers in the 1840s seems to have been in tobacco. In September 1844 Excise Officers heard of a cargo of tobacco being landed at Huttoft. The cargo was tracked inland from the coast and intercepted as it travelled to Lincoln in a cart. The young man in charge put up a fight and knocked down Officer Beech before making his escape, but the Excise officers had captured 730*lbs* of illegally imported tobacco.

They locked the tobacco up at the Monson Arms in Lincoln and sold the captured horse and cart for £28. Unfortunately the tobacco was promptly stolen! The smuggling gang was hard to capture, but Joseph Clark of Lincoln and William Radford of Newark were each fined £100 for 'aiding and abetting delivery' of smuggled goods. In August 1846 five tons of tobacco were seized on the coast.

Of course much of the smuggling that took place was on a smaller scale, involving a few minor items brought ashore illegally by sailors and fishermen. Sometimes people even 'smuggled' goods ashore accidentally! In October 1842 a Mr Bass, the master of the steam packet 'Mercury,' was tried at Gainsborough for smuggling a bottle of brandy ashore. It turned out that the offending bottle was a present for Bass that had been left on the cabin table for him by a passenger, evidence to this effect being given by Mrs Williamson the stewardess. Bass had brought the bottle ashore and, despite many character witnesses, he had to pay the minimum fine for the offence (£100). He wrote out a cheque before leaving the courtroom.

A more guilty character was James O'Donnell of the 'Wakefield.' In 1868 he was fined £1 9s. 0d. for smuggling tobacco and cigars ashore in the lining of his coat. Thus the image of the 'romantic' smuggler was reduced to that of a penny-pinching petty criminal by the mid-century.

The problem with some people was that they did not want to go to sea at all. Many boys were apprenticed to Grimsby fishermen, but conditions could be harsh. In December 1861 all three apprentices of Grimsby smack-owner John Hill absconded rather than go to sea with him again. They were brought before Spilsby magistrates and given two or three weeks' hard labour instead. Cases like this occurred frequently: in January 1874 Grimsby apprentice J. W. Pearman made his seventh court appearance for refusing to go to sea, receiving a gaol sentence of 28 days.

It is not surprising that apprentices behaved like this if the masters were like the aptly-named William Brusey, who was charged with manslaughter on the high seas in March 1874. Brusey was captain of a fishing smack that had sailed from Grimsby to Flamborough Head in August 1873, when he beat apprentice William Parker on the hand for burning the fish that he was cooking. The boy was so upset that he leapt into the sea and was drowned. The case against Brusey was dismissed, but it is doubtful whether he secured a replacement apprentice.

Life on board was often fairly rough - even when in dock. In January 1874 John Mooney, a crewman on the smack 'Surprise,' got into an argument with one of his colleagues while they were tied up in the fish dock. It was Mooney who surprised his opponent by drawing a knife and stabbing the man in the leg, an assault for which he was fined 21s.

A typical Grimsby fishing boat of the late nineteenth century
Courtesy Grimsby Library

Robbery from a boat was fairly rare apart from cases of pilfering in the docks. A case of theft occurred on the Trent in January 1862 when a barge loaded with potatoes was left unattended at Crowgarth near Gainsborough while its crew went off for their lunch. Three men on another barge that was passing by laden with bricks took the opportunity to remove some of the potatoes. The sentences handed out were very considerable: four years' penal servitude, a year of hard labour and six months' hard labour.

In June 1862 George Dunston got into trouble for the illegal removal of a boat at the Brayford Pool in Lincoln. The boat in question had been moored at the wharf by Robert Cook but its position made it impossible for George Dunston to get his father's boat to the wharf. He broke the lock on Cook's boat and left it drifting in the Pool, for which he was fined 2s. damages and 43s. costs.

The actual theft of a boat occurred in June 1893 when George Cox, a lad of sixteen, and William Smith, only fourteen, commandeered the steam tug 'Star' and took it out from Grimsby for a voyage into the Humber. The boys had been out at 11.30pm at night in the Fish Dock and broke into the tug's engine room. They lit the fires and got up steam, getting out of the dock by telling the gateman they were 'going round to the other dock.'

The next morning the 'Star' was seen by the Killingholme coastguard to be ashore on the Yorkshire side (no 'Humberside' then), and later in the day it was seen to be ashore on the Lincolnshire side! While this was going on, the 'Star' had actually been passed by the 'Lady Bute,' on board which was Smith's father, who had shouted to his errant son to wait until he returned later to help them. However, Coastguard Evans boarded the 'Star' as unmanageable and found two lads who excused their plight by saying there was a boiler problem.

Evans inspected the 'Star' and found there was indeed a boiler problem: there was no water left in it but the boys had kept a roaring fire going. The boiler was in considerable danger and much damage had been done. Evans took the two boys ashore but they ran off, though they were arrested later. They excused themselves by saying they had intended going out for a 'pleasure trip,' but each had to enjoy a month of hard labour; presumably they were Victorian Grimsby's idea of joy-riders.

Moving only a short distance away from the sea to the actual coast, we find slightly different examples of criminal activity. Skegness was hardly Monte Carlo or even Las Vegas, especially not in January 1874, but PC Morritt clearly thought he had uncovered a major gambling den at the Sea View Hotel. He made an impromptu visit to the opening ceremony of the hotel's new extension, and found a raffle taking place for the 50 guests with prizes of beer and liquor. Two little girls were drawing numbers from a bag. The owner of the hotel, Susannah Morley, was charged with allowing gaming on her premises but contended that the building was not hers but next to hers and that the raffle had been organised by the builders. The case was dismissed.

CHAPTER 5: FRAUD AND FAKE

One of the most common types of fraud in Victorian Britain was 'smashing' - the manufacture and passing of fake coins. There seems to have been a core of criminals who did most of the manufacturing, favouring coins of middling value. Many others, however, were involved in the passing of the coins and these were the people most likely to be arrested.

A rare example of an actual 'smasher' being caught occurred at Barton in 1847. David Worrill bought tea and tobacco with fake shillings and, when his house was searched, a mould was found. Worrill protested that he had found the mould in a dyke, but this lame excuse did not protect him from a sentence of seven years' transportation.

A number of those involved in this racket were arrested several times for similar offences. In January 1855 John Jackson tried to buy ½lb of ham in Lincoln with a fake half-crown. His protestations that he didn't realise the coin was a fake were weakened by the information that he had only recently left prison after enduring a period in Her Majesty's care for a similar crime. The following week three men were tried at Louth for passing fake half-crowns at Horncastle in December 1854; they received a year's hard labour apiece.

Fake coins were so common that they were almost a way of life; they were also easily detectable, but nonetheless foolhardy souls continued to think that they could get away with passing a fake shilling or two. Thus it was that in February 1862 a young woman named Keziah Franklin tried to buy ale at The Bell in Spalding with a fake shilling. The landlord, who was clearly used to this sort of thing, tested the coin in a very basic way: he bent it. Franklin's shilling proved to be made of pewter, but rather surprisingly she put it back in her pocket and went off to the shop of John Cox.

The foolish woman asked Cox to change the shilling for two sixpences, which he did, but subsequently found the coin to be a fake. Keziah Franklin came back later and tried to give him a proper shilling instead, but by then it was too late to regret the offence. She received a year's hard labour.

At Grantham in March 1862, William Brown added to the crime of faking a coin by trying to pass himself off in an unlikely identity. He claimed that his name was Samuel Brownlow, though it is to be doubted that the family at Belton House welcomed him into their arms. Brown was at Grantham buttermarket on 8th March and his behaviour attracted the attention of the police, who watched him. He bought 1lb of butter for 1s. 5d. from Mrs Hamilton of Barkston, but the coin he gave her was a fake florin. The police seized him and found three other fakes in his possession. Brown claimed that he had been tricked into taking the coins in exchange for a neckcloth and a knife, but in 1856 he had been convicted of passing fake coins at Nottingham and had received a year in prison. On this occasion he was sentenced to three years' penal servitude.

Passing fake coinage was just one way in which the wheels of Victorian commerce were oiled by the wiles of the criminal classes. Fraud was also common, and it came in many guises, some unbelievably simple, some even quite comic. An example of the latter was Arthur Wyndham, who came to Grantham in January 1874. He claimed to be Henry Atkinson, advertising agent for an unlikely troupe of acrobats called the London Combination Company. He announced that the acrobats would be performing six nights in Grantham and booked himself into the Chequers Inn, where he enjoyed a good dinner, a brandy, a nice bed and a hearty breakfast, all 'on account.' Then he promptly vanished, getting as far as Newark before the authorities caught up with him.

Cheques were often involved in forgery and fraud, being relatively easy to misuse. At Grantham in January 1862 John Charles succeeded — temporarily — in extracting £105 9s. from maltster Robert Lee in the form of a cheque made out to 'Mr Hack or bearer.' Lee was a Spittlegate maltster who had received a consignment of barley from Mr Hack, a Willoughby farmer. Charles had met Hack's waggoner at a hostelry in Little Gonerby, where he had shown great interest in the load of barley. Armed with the exact information he needed, Charles had found it easy to convince Lee's clerk to let him have the cheque. With the cheque cashed, Charles went out and bought a horse for £7 10s. which he rode home to Welby. When arrested, he was found in possession of a large number of banknotes. He was given three years penal servitude, having previously served fifteen months' for the theft of two horses.

On 9th August 1865 William Bird forged a £27 cheque at Boston, which landed him in trouble for various technical legal reasons. Bird bought a mare from a farmer at Moulton for £27 which was to be delivered to Spalding for a farmer named Plowright. He got Plowright to make out a cheque for the money, payable to the other man, but then cashed it himself by endorsing it with his signature on the back. Bird's purpose for doing this seems to have been highly confused, since he gave the cash back to Plowright later the same day. Although he had obviously not stolen anything he had made a false signature on the back of the cheque and so was guilty of fraud. He had to go to prison for the requisite fifteen months!

Of course a 'cheque' in those days was often not a printed document as it is today. In fact it functioned in much the same way as the traditional 'written request for payment.' In November 1867 farmer William Ducking sent one of his workers, William Mayhew, to Horncastle to sell a horse. He was given a note asking the landlady of the Greyhound Inn to provide him with some cash. The landlady, Fanny Marshall, read the note — which functioned like a cheque — and was not impressed by a scrawled message at the bottom: 'Please give bearer 6s.' She suspected that this message was in a different handwriting and had been added by the bearer himself, so that poor Mayhew ended up in court on a serious charge. He escaped with a not guilty verdict, but it demonstrated how confusing the system could be.

A whole variety of techniques were used by various characters to trick money out of people. It was quite clear from the way some of these crimes were organised that they were bound to be discovered in the end. An example was Joseph Husband, originally a Scothern man, who at 34 was still living with his mother although she had gone to live in Nettleham with her new farmer husband. Joseph went to the Nettleham grocer, William Dawkins, with an order for 18s. worth of goods that he said was from his mother. When Dawkins sent in his account it was discovered that the order was a forgery, so Joseph Husband appeared in court with his mother as the main prosecution witness. His defence was that he had been misled by his mother and abused by his step-father, who had trumped up the case to get rid of him. They succeeded in this: he went to prison for three months.

A common means of obtaining money through false pretences was to collect for charity when the 'charity' actually began literally at home. Walter Wood received a month's hard labour after tricking Thomas Dyson out of 2s. 6d. at Gainsborough in February 1893. He had been going around collecting for the rather diverse interests of Morton St Paul's Cricket Club and Dr Barnardo's.

In January 1884 Mary Hare of Ulceby answered her door to a stranger named George Marshall, who said he was a County Court bailiff levying a 'distress rate' to help the poor in a very bad winter. She gave him 5s. as requested, but in fact it was so dark that she had really given him 2d. Nonetheless it was not Mary Hare who got into trouble, but George Marshall: he was no bailiff, just a villain indulging in a little private enterprise. He was given four months' hard labour.

THREATENING LETTERS.

BRIGG, BARTON, CAISTOR, GRIMSBY, KIRTON, AND
WINTERTON INCENDIARY FIRE ASSOCIATION.

£50 REWARD !

WHEREAS Mr. HENRY BARKER, of BURTON-UPON-STATHER, Mr. WILLIAM CHAPMAN, of WINTRINGHAM, and Mr. JOHN SCARBOROUGH, of WINTRINGHAM, Members of this Association, have severally received, from some person or persons unknown, LETTERS, threatening to set fire to their Property.

NOTICE IS HEREBY GIVEN,

That a Reward of **FIFTY** POUNDS will be paid to any person or persons giving such information as shall lead to the conviction of the sender or senders of such Threatening Letters, or of any one of them.

Any person or persons giving **PRIVATE INFORMATION**, which may be useful in leading to the detection of the offender or offenders, to the Secretaries, or to the Superintendent of Police at Winterton, or the Superintendent of Police at Brigg, will be liberally remunerated, according to the value of the information given, which will be considered as strictly confidential.

The above Reward of **FIFTY** POUNDS will be paid on conviction, and will be apportioned in such manner as the Committee of the Association shall determine.

BY ORDER

HETT, FREER, & HETT,

Brigg, 8th December, 1864.   Treasurers and Secretaries.

W. CRESSEY, PRINTER, BOOKSELLER AND STATIONER, POST OFFICE, BRIGG.

During 1864 North Lincolnshire was struck by incendiaries and threatening letters. Landowners offered rewards for information
Lincolnshire Police Museum

A much cleverer scheme was organised by John Fisher of Grantham during 1893. Fisher watched out for newspaper adverts from women housekeepers seeking work. He then wrote to them, giving a Spalding address. He asked each one for references and a 5s. deposit upon which he would send the money for their train journey to meet him in Spalding. Such exploitation of trusting women servants seems, somehow, to be a typical Victorian crime.

A similar form of ruse landed a man from Beverley in trouble when complaints were made at Kirton-in-Lindsey about his counting competition. John Bray advertised a competition in the press, with prizes like a bicycle, sewing-machine and a watch. Contestants had to give the number of As and Es in a chapter of Isaiah and pay the entry fee of a shilling. Of course a large number were told that they had 'won' and were requested to send another shilling to cover the carriage and packing of their 'prize.' Nothing was ever delivered, and it seems to have been Bray's Lincolnshire customers who were the first to complain.

There were also a number of frauds that fell within the bracket of commercial trickery. This was especially easy when it is realised that a lot of the trade in the agricultural economy involved informal wheeling and dealing. An example can be seen in the behaviour of a horse dealer named George West at the Lincoln fair in July 1877. West came from Epsom in Surrey and was left with a fairly useless brown mare that he did not want to take back with him. Thomas Aslin of Washingborough showed an interest in the horse, so to encourage him in a purchase West claimed to be the farmer of 1,300 acres near Billinghay and said that he was the nephew of Aslin's neighbour. West also said that he was keen to sell his horse to a Lincolnshire man as he was local himself.

Nearly everything West told Aslin was a lie, but the Washingborough man did not know this and agreed to pay £31 for the horse. He had already made a deposit of £25 when a vet, Mr Hicks, inspected the horse and declared it to be 'a perfect screw' — useless — and not worth £5. West was arrested and his claims proved to be false. The horse's history was discussed in court; it had belonged to a man in Rouen who had sold it to a Hastings cabman for £20, from whom West had bought it for £24. West's attempt at cutting a fast bargain cost him two months in prison.

Selling a bad horse in the guise of a good horse was a rather more common offence than selling a bad acrobat in the guise of a good one! However, in July 1892 William Blumenfeld was charged before Lincoln magistrates with gaining 1s. by false pretences. He had published a handbill saying that 'Herr Sandow, conqueror of Samson...' would be appearing at the Corn Exchange. Sandow was a very famous acrobat, but the audience did not see Sandow at all but William Blumenfeld instead. The latter defended himself by saying 'I do a better performance than Sandow.' He was found guilty but judgment was deferred.

A different form of commercial fraud was perpetrated by Edward Frayne in Cleethorpes in 1895. Frayne was a collector for the Royal London Insurance Company and could claim a share of any new business that he brought in. He was not very successful at canvassing for trade, but made up three 'clients' and claimed a royalty for starting new accounts. He was given three months' hard labour.

A number of cases occurred where people were accused of concealing their assets when made bankrupt. This crime became more common after bankruptcy ceased to be an offence for which a person could be imprisoned. One case in 1884 involved a Boston cattle-dealer, Arthur Clarke, who was charged at Bourne with unlawfully concealing and fraudulently removing £500 just before he became bankrupt. It was alleged that he had bought £600 worth of stock just before his bankruptcy and taken it to London, from which it was believed he had made £60 profit that had not been declared as an asset.

Clarke contended that he had lost the money after an evening of doubtful activity. He had met two men 'in the road' and gone to a pub with them, after which they all visited a house of ill-fame near King's Cross before going to the theatre. At some stage in all this Clarke claimed to have lost his money. The Bourne magistrates were unimpressed and sent him to the Assizes.

At the Assizes in May 1884 Clarke was found guilty and sentenced to two months' prison. It was proved that he had bought cattle and sheep for £929, mostly paid for on credit, and sold them at an unknown profit. He had paid off £385 of his debts and then bought about seventy sheep at Stamford for around £600; it was these that had been sold in London with the profit being 'lost.' The court was not convinced by his excuse.

Perhaps it was a reflection of the depression that agriculture was going through, but there was a rash of cases like Clarke's at this time. Charles Goddard was a farmer at Butterwick near Boston who, by the end of 1883, was in severe financial trouble with liabilities of over £500. On 19th January 1884 he sold off his farm and stock, moving into the house of Samuel Strawson who had bought some of Goddard's goods for £150 and also received £100 for his troubles. Goddard then left for Liverpool, where he was expecting to take passage for the USA. He was instead arrested there for fraudulent concealment of £100, the sum he had given to Strawson, and sentenced to eight months' hard labour.

A form of fraud was perjury (deliberate lying in a court). A topic that was often linked with perjury was illegitimacy, for there seems to have been a good deal of uncertainty in at least some minds when it came to a question of parentage. Thus Maria Drayton, a pauper from Horncastle, alleged that her child derived from the attentions of Mr Holmes, the Master of Horncastle workhouse. She had been a pauper in the workhouse and had left to go into domestic service at New Bolingbroke, but she had suddenly given birth and her new employer had refused all wages. Following this she had accused Holmes of being the father; this would have been a popular move with some, since workhouses were then at their most unpopular. However, Drayton found few who would believe her.

The penalties for perjury could be severe. Gainsborough butcher Herbert Gambles was given three years' penal servitude in 1895 for lying to the magistrates over an illegitimacy case. Mary Killelay had had a child and had sworn to the magistrates that Gambles was the father; this was an important consideration due to paternity fees being payable. Gambles denied it, and also denied offering marriage; however, Mary's sister claimed he had offered marriage in July 1894 and admitted parenthood in May 1895, even offering to pay 3s. 6d. a week costs. It was because he kept none of these offers that the case was brought before the magistrates. Gambles claimed that he lied on his first court appearance as he was 'mazzled' after three days of drinking, but the Assize judge took a dim view of his behaviour.

1876 drawing of a Lincolnshire policeman
Lincolnshire Police Museum

CHAPTER SIX:
CRIMES OF THE COUNTRYSIDE

1. Poaching

Two developments of former years conspired to make poaching one of the most fraught issues in the Victorian countryside. These were the spread of enclosures, especially during the period 1793-1815, which deprived many rural families of the traditional source of wild meat, the common; the other was the arrival of the Game Laws in the 1820s, giving the landowners stringent new powers in the resulting battle against the poachers.

Thus Lincolnshire courts saw an almost endless stream of poaching offences; some minor, some very serious indeed. 'Trespass in search of game' was as common as traffic offences are today and was generally punished fairly lightly: Thomas Dolby of Gelston was fined £1 at Grantham in January 1855 and Richard Alman of Washingborough paid exactly the same fine at Lincoln a decade later. However, two men arrested for 'night-poaching,' which was technically a different offence, at Dunston in 1868 received two months' hard labour each.

Poaching attracted much more attention when the nightly battles of wits between poachers and gamekeepers threatened to boil over into actual bodily violence. This could happen on both sides, for gamekeepers were often unpopular and ostracised, while some poachers were prepared to use violence to escape capture.

At Corringham on 1st March 1866 three men were out 'night-poaching' on the lands of Sir Thomas Beckett of Somerby Park, though it says a lot about Victorian tenancy agreements that the fields were rented out to Henry Northings while under the supervision of Beckett's gamekeeper. At 2.45am the gamekeeper, John Bartrop, had edged his way to within six feet of the poachers and hid himself in a hedge. Choosing his moment for maximum surprise, Bartrop suddenly leapt out from the hedge and said, 'Good morning my lads,' to the poachers.

William Wells, one of the gang, reacted angrily, 'Stand back you b.... or I'll blow your b.... brains out!' The three men ran off into Lea Wood but Bartrop contacted the police and the Turk's Head, a notorious Gainsborough pub, was searched. Wells was found there with gun caps in his pocket, which he claimed were for 'blowing out candles.' The guns were found in the house of another poacher, Gilbert.

The third man was caught later and, with Wells and Gilbert, was charged with poaching and also the theft of two coats. Sentences varied between six months' and ten years' penal servitude, the latter for Wells as he had already been convicted of a felony.

A few months later William Quickfall was spotted in Hazel Lane near Crowle at five o'clock in the morning. Quickfall had gone into a field and was carrying a gun, but PC John Waddington decided to confront him. Quickfall's pockets were so full of game that he could not run away, but he pointed the gun at Waddington and threatened to shoot him. When Waddington persisted in his efforts, Quickfall shot him in the arm and then threatened to shoot him in the head. Waddington had to have his arm amputated. Quickfall's defence that he was shooting crows was rejected, but due to his age (he was 63) he received only five years' penal servitude.

The poacher's friend, the rabbit's enemy:
A gin trap in the Lincolnshire Police Museum

A typical poaching fracas that could easily have had serious consequences occurred in the woods near Burwell on 23rd December 1867. This was a classic time for a poaching 'affray', just before Christmas. That poaching activity was expected can be seen from the fact that at 2.30am three policemen were on duty in a plantation when they heard a gunshot. They followed the steps of four men along Cow Dyke Lane and then PC Edward Hudson turned his light on.

The poachers reacted quickly, James Paddison telling Isaac Dowse to shoot at the constable, though in fact Dowse just threatened him with his gun. Two other policemen then tried to arrest Paddison, who hit at them with his stick, whereupon the officers gave him a sound beating. Dowse was chased by Hudson, but turned and shot at him; the other poachers escaped, leaving 35 rabbits and three pheasants behind.

Paddison and Dowse were charged with attempting to kill PC Hudson, but blamed another poacher for firing the gun. They were found guilty of shooting without intent to kill, Dowse receiving a sentence of fifteen months and Paddison one of a year.

By far the most famous Lincolnshire poaching case of the Victorian era was one which ended in the death of Henry Walker, a gamekeeper on Viscount St Vincent's estate at Norton Disney. Early in 1877, on a cold winter night, Henry Walker had confronted a gang of poachers at a plantation on Stapleford Moor; he had been shot in the legs at a range of about twelve yards, and was taken home to die. Quick work by the police resulted in the arrest of William Fletcher, a notorious young poacher, in Newark; he was taken to the bedroom of the dying gamekeeper, and was identified. Two other men were arrested in Newark.

At first it seemed that the case was settled, but one of the poachers, George Garner, told a different story. He said that the murderous shot had been fired by 'Slenderman,' also known as William Clark, and that the villain was still at large. Garner stated that he wanted to make this clear in case one of the 'innocent' was executed for Clark's offence. Mrs Fletcher also testified that her husband had gone poaching with 'Slenderman.'

A reward of £10 was offered for information that would help the police to capture Clark, but this had to be increased to £20 and then £50. Superintendent Brown was put on the trail, but he had only a young recruit to assist him. They went to Hull, Grimsby and Yarmouth without success, and then went to Lowestoft. There Brown and his recruit searched the area without any real help from the local police, but one evening Brown spotted 'Slenderman' drinking at the White Horse Inn with several other men. Fearing trouble if he attempted an arrest on his own, Brown sent the recruit off to get reinforcements and Clark was captured. When charged, he simply remarked, 'Oh, indeed.' He was found to have pawned his gun in Lowestoft High Street.

Clark's appearance at the magistrates excited great interest. Although he had a variety of aliases, including Western, Burk, Ross, Gray and Willis, he was a native of Norton Disney. A charge of wilful murder was recorded against Clark and George Garner, and they were sent to the Assize in March 1877.

At the trial Garner did all he could to lay the blame on Clark. He claimed that 'Slenderman' had tried to kill him too and he had had to plead for his life on bended knee, saying 'Don't shoot, for God's sake don't shoot.' Garner was acquitted, but Clark did not escape. His defence argued that William Fletcher had shot the gamekeeper, and it was known that Fletcher had been to prison three times and prosecuted on another seven occasions for assault and poaching. When called to give evidence, Fletcher 'seemed to treat the matter in a jocular light' and was censured by the judge. Nonetheless Clark was sentenced to hang and when asked to comment only said, 'I did not fire the shot.' 'Slenderman' was executed on 29th March.

In early February 1874 the *Lincolnshire Chronicle* tried to whip up some excitement about the poachers by reporting that 'Neither fur nor feather, domestic or wild, is safe from their clutches, provided it can be stowed in the pocket.' They reported on an outbreak of poaching over the New Year period (it was also a notoriously seasonal practice, with Christmas an especial problem!). Two men named Wiles and Williams were charged with poaching in a turnip field beside 'Old Bloxholme Road' at Mere. Both had guns and dogs, while Williams had already served six months for poaching pigeons. This time they were fined £5 each.

A little further north-west two other men named Ramshaw and Massey went out poaching at Doddington Park with four dogs, one of which was a lurcher. They were spotted by a gamekeeper who sent for the police, and a search of their pockets revealed a rabbit (dead but still warm), two ferrets and a special collapsible poaching spade that could be hidden in a pocket. They were fined £4 and £3 respectively.

Poaching was a dangerous offence, not only because of the battles it inspired, but because it involved the use of guns under less than ideal conditions. It proved fatal for a poacher named Walker or 'Pyewipe' near

Photograph of supposed beadle and poacher at Gainthorpe in c.1860
Courtesy Welholme Galleries, Grimsby

Bardney in 1837, for he stooped to adjust the wire of a snare-gun he was setting and shot himself in the face. His accomplice ran for help, but wouldn't say where he had left the dying man, presumably for fear of prosecution. Pyewipe was eventually found, but his faithful dog was by his side and would let no stranger approach. Not until after the dog had been secured was the poacher found to be on the verge of death, and indeed he passed away very soon afterwards.

Gamekeepers had to be trustworthy men, for their position gave them a good deal of responsibility and some could be bribed to 'be somewhere else' at an opportune time. There were also suspicions that gamekeepers indulged in a little freelance poaching of their own, for they had an ideal excuse for being out at night with a shotgun. In the Scrivelsby game case of 1867, John Dymoke brought his own gamekeeper to court on a charge of defrauding his employer. John Kenyon, the gamekeeper, was expected to shoot game and send it to Lincoln, thus adding to the income of the Dymoke family. John Dymoke believed that Kenyon's accounts of the game that had been shot were 'light,' and linked this with two hampers sent to London by Kenyon. In court it was proved that Kenyon had indeed sent two hampers of hares to London just before Christmas, but the prosecution was unable to prove that the hares had belonged to Dymoke.

Poachers were not only interested in fowl, of course, but even the humble rabbit. In 1877 Joseph Jevitt was the Great Northern Railway's signalman at Donington-on-Bain, where he could see lots of rabbits in the field beside the railway line. Unable to resist the temptation, he set ten traps to catch them, but it was Jevitt that was caught when his footsteps were traced from the illegal traps back to the signalbox. He was given six weeks' hard labour.

A few weeks after this an even more pathetic case of 'poaching' occurred at Tumby. Sir Henry Hawley's gamekeeper brought four people to court for gathering lilies in Fulsby Wood without permission. They were fined 6d. each, with an extra 9s. 6d. for costs!

There were a number of traditions about shooting and hunting that led to confusion, which in some cases could be very embarrassing. In April 1884 a policeman, a publican and the manager of a Scunthorpe ironworks all appeared in court for shooting game on the Earl of Yarborough's estate without a licence. The charge against the constable had to be withdrawn as it was found he was giving evidence against the other two. It was all part of a 'pick-up day' shoot which the constable had been watching; he had been invited to join in and had done so, but he then 'turned informer.' The two men denied shooting game and said they had shot rabbits with the gamekeeper's permission, but they were still fined £5 each.

2. Stealing Animals

The name of 'poaching' can be applied to the practice of stealing wild creatures by shooting them and stowing them surreptitiously into a pocket. But the depredation of the animal kingdom extended also to more domesticated farm animals and the chief attraction among these was the sheep.

Although many poachers went about their practice at least partially because it was exciting, the humble sheep was more often the victim of the starving or desperate. Because of this, the theft of mutton or lamb can be seen as the typical crime of the rural poor, and one that was notoriously difficult to prevent.

Occasionally, though, sheep stealing was a more organised practice and this made it easier to detect, for a group of people were much more likely to leave evidence behind them. Thus it was that on 3rd May 1847 Mr Todd of Hemingby found the remains of one of his sheep: the head, skin and entrails had been left, but all the meat had gone. The footsteps of three men could be traced going off towards Horncastle, but although Mr Todd offered a reward of five guineas he can have had little hope of actually catching anyone. Nonetheless, he took a plaster cast of the footprints just in case.

A week later, by an amazing coincidence, he saw a similar footprint to one of those by the dead sheep. He traced the steps to a nearby house and arranged for it to be searched. Inside was uncovered a veritable Aladdin's cave of stolen goods: some meat from the dead sheep, some fowls, a bucket stolen from the Crown Inn, an iron basin and a stolen mop. There was even a sack of potatoes that had been stolen from a poor man at West Ashby. Two men were arrested and their wives were traced to Belchford where they were also brought into custody. It was found that the contents of the entire house were stolen, even including a wooden tub and brushes stolen from a local druggist. So on this occasion a stolen sheep led to the uncovering of a real gang of rural criminals.

3. Incendiarism

Incendiarism was the Victorian name for arson, the crime that most terrified Lincolnshire's farmers. Farms were notoriously exposed to the attack of the arsonist as haystacks and barns could contain the fruits of a year's labours, yet could be destroyed in two hours. They were also difficult to protect and often beyond the useful range of any fire brigade.

In 1830-1831 there had been an especially bad outbreak of incendiarism and 'rick-burning,' part of which had been blamed on the mythical Captain Swing. On 29th July 1831 Richard Cooling and Thomas Mottley were executed for a series of arson attacks on stacks and farm buildings in the Kirkby and Hagnaby district. Incendiarist attacks continued intermittently until the end of the century, often focussing on unpopular farmers or ones that employed machinery to replace men.

In December 1839 a farmer at South Thoresby, near Louth, was attacked. He lost a stack of wheat and two of oats, valued at £250, but was protected by insurance. No-one was caught, and such a failure was fairly typical. For anyone who was caught, punishment could be severe: two youths received 15 years' transportation for burning down a stack in 1847.

In November 1855 Mr Slight of Waddington lost two stacks worth £105. Typically, the loss could have been prevented had there been a nearby supply of water. A man named Freeman, who was a tramp, was arrested but there was insufficient evidence to find him guilty of the arson attack. Instead, he was given three months in prison for being 'a rogue and a vagabond.' Strangers and tramps were generally high on the list of suspects for incendiarism, often without any good reason except the suspicion of strangers.

On 8th September 1861 fire broke out in a stackyard at Belton belonging to Robert Robinson. It was 2am, so help was slow in arriving and Robinson lost three stacks altogether. A number of villagers turned out to help and one of these was Thomas Cawkwell who, although fairly drunk, helped for over three hours.

After the fire had been put out footsteps leading away from the stackyard were found in a field of mangold-wurzel. These matched Cawkwell's boots and, since he was known to have a grudge against Robinson, he was arrested.

Cawkwell had been courting one of Robinson's female servants, Charlotte Booth, and had been thrown out of the farmhouse twice. The Belton blacksmith claimed that he had heard Cawkwell promise to 'do' Robinson, but doubt was cast on this evidence as the blacksmith had been in prison at least five times for being drunk. The judge also had a problem with Cawkwell's father who had been too drunk to talk to the police when they had questioned him; he was paid back by being refused his travel expenses to the trial in Lincoln. Cawkwell was found guilty and sentenced to twelve years' penal servitude despite the jury's plea for mercy on the grounds of provocation.

FREE  PARDON.

ARSON
IN
NORTH LINCOLNSHIRE.

WHEREAS Fires have lately occurred on the premises of Mr. JOHN STEPHENSON of Thornton Curtis, Messrs. HUNTSMAN of Barton-upon-Humber, Mr. EDMUND DAVY of Worlaby, and Mr. JOSEPH JOHNSON of Appleby, all in the County of Lincoln, which are believed to have been caused by Incendiaries.

NOTICE IS HEREBY GIVEN, THAT

HER MAJESTY'S
PARDON

Will be granted to any Accomplice (not being the person who actually set fire to the property) who shall give such information and evidence as shall lead to the discovery and conviction of the Incendiary or Incendiaries in any of the cases above mentioned.

BY ORDER,

JOHN HETT,
Clerk to the Justices acting at Brigg.

Brigg, 7th February, 1865.

WILLIAM CRESSEY, PRINTER, BOOKSELLER AND STATIONER, BRIGG.

A poster of February 1865 issued as part of the campaign against arson
Lincolnshire Police Museum

Grudges between farmworkers and their employers were often the reason for a fire, especially where the workers were employed on temporary jobs. On 5th September 1865 some stacks were destroyed by fire at Whaplode, causing about £50 worth of damage. Thomas Robinson, a young farm labourer, helped to put the fire out but was arrested soon after and accused of incendiarism. His brother Jonathan gave evidence that he had seen Thomas with a newspaper soaked in saltpetre and water. Thomas had said, 'I'll show you how it will act on a stack.' He also stole his brother's matches.

Thomas Robinson had then gone out, returning at about 10pm in a confused state. The stacks, only 120 yards from the Robinsons' cottage, were alight by this time. 'I did it,' Thomas said to Jonathan, 'and if you split I will shoot you dead.' However, it took Jonathan a month to give evidence against his brother and it was suggested that he was motivated by the £20 reward. Thomas was given five years' penal servitude but his brother was refused the reward on the grounds of being an accomplice.

The spread of 'lucifer' matches was another common cause of fire. Twelve-year-old Thomas Tollieday set fire to Richard Knight's hovel at Long Sutton on 14th August 1865 when he experimented with what a match could do. His mother told him to blame 'Thickpenny's girl' but he was found not guilty of criminal intent in any case.

Bad feeling between a farmer and one of his household servants was suspected of being the motive for a fire at Laughton on 29th July 1873. Martha Clarke sent her employer, farmer Charles Howsham, to Cold Harbour on what turned out to be a 'fool's errand.' While he was away a fire started and he suspected Clarke of having started it. Martha contended that a man had come to the house in the farmer's absence and broken a window, then striking her with a stick. Evidence was produced to show that the window had been broken from the inside, but there were no grounds to convict Miss Clarke of the fire.

Another case of bad feeling led to a fire at Pinchbeck in February 1868. John Welsch had been drinking at the Pole Hole, where he nursed bitter feelings about farmer William Robertson who had refused to employ him. Then he went on to the Wheat Sheaf, only two hundred yards from Robertson's wheat stack which mysteriously caught fire later that evening, half an hour after Welsch had left the pub. He was given 18 months' hard labour. This sentence remained fairly standard for the offence for the rest of the century.

Some people chose unusual objects for their incendiarist attentions. In January 1874 George Laming set fire to a manure heap at Wootton Wold near Barton-on-Humber. He could only offer the lame excuse that he 'wanted a blaze.' A heap of manure was apparently worth £10.

Three criminals from the archive of the
Lincolnshire Police Museum

CHAPTER SEVEN: POVERTY

Social services in Victorian Lincolnshire were very few; indeed, they were dominated by the procedures established by the 1834 Poor Law Amendment Act which had stipulated that all the able-bodied poor should be offered 'relief' in the workhouse and nothing outside of it. In fact the workhouses of Lincolnshire were never capacious enough to accommodate even a fraction of the county's paupers, but many others decided voluntarily to do almost anything they could to stay outside of the 'new Bastilles.'

Many of the poor managed to eke out some form of living by begging, and they were joined in this by the large numbers of itinerant workers who were not averse to begging as a means of subsidising their journeys. Magistrates throughout the country battled continuously against this unofficial sub-economy, with little success; settlements on major roads, such as Grantham, were always popular with beggars and tramps.

Tramps could secure a night's accommodation and a meal if they applied to the Master of the local workhouse, who would expect some work in return. This often involved hard physical labour and was a source of many complaints. In December 1839 the Master of the Boston workhouse, Mr Silvester, brought one of his overnight 'guests' up before the magistrates. James Melson had enjoyed bed and breakfast at the expense of the Boston ratepayers, but had then refused to do the two hours work stipulated by the rules.

Silvester had accosted Melson, but the tramp had not been cowed at all: he had made a speech to the other tramps, saying that none of them had gone there to work for 'rascals' but to be decently fed and treated! The result was that all the other 'guests' refused to work too. Melson was sentenced to fourteen days in prison (also provided at the ratepayers' expense), whereupon the other rebellious tramps decided that they would do their work after all. The *Chronicle* chose to print this story alongside a report that a lad from the Lincoln parish of St Botolph's had lived entirely off begging for three years, and had done so well that he was getting married. However it was not always so easy. The Mayor of Louth ordered his police to arrest all beggars who came into the town. Yet even the Louth workhouse had problems, for example, in 1847 tramp Charles Kemp was given a week in prison after refusing to do his share of stone breaking.

One of the reasons that tramps were so disliked was because they had a reputation for being thieves. It was certainly fairly easy for a tramp to steal on his journey; if he could get away from the district with his thievings, then he was likely to escape detection altogether. However, getting away was not always easy: George Woods was arrested at Billinghay in June 1846 after he stole four umbrellas while passing through the village. He had a previous conviction for a similar offence at Sleaford and so was transported for seven years. At the same Kesteven Sessions another tramp, Alex Cunningham, received a similar sentence for stealing a watch from the Metheringham surgeon.

Some more sophisticated beggars tried to get money from people by claiming all forms of misfortune and family disaster. In June 1847 Edward Rudgard took part in a scheme to defraud charitable local people by making up a false petition. He and a few helpers claimed that a widow named Mrs Hardy had six children, of whom the eldest was blind. The widow wanted to send her son to a Bristol asylum for the blind, but needed money. Rudgard produced a forged certificate from the boy's physician and, to add credence, placed the names of a few local dignitaries on the petition as having donated money. The police, however, had difficulty catching the practitioners of this typical Victorian crime.

In June 1847 a woman called at Gate Burton Hall near Gainsborough. A servant girl was bringing her into the house when the woman's face suddenly turned black as she was taken over by a powerful fit. She fell to the floor, her face turning white then black again, and her limbs becoming rigid. The servants were terrified, but the woman gradually recovered. She was given a brandy and a good meal to restore her. At this point another servant, who had just moved to Gate Burton from a position near Newark, came into the room and recognised the woman as having played the same trick at the house where she had worked previously. The woman and her accomplice were given a month in gaol to contemplate the error of their ways.

In January 1855 the people of Moulton were going to church when they passed a rather dishevelled woman with three children. Just as the church bell started to ring, the woman fell down in a fit. One or two charitable souls gave her some money to comfort her in her troubles. A few hours later the good people of neighbouring Weston were coming out of their church, when the same woman had a fit in front of them. This was too much of a coincidence for one of the Weston people, who happened to have witnessed the first performance at Moulton, and he protested. The erstwhile invalid made a hasty exit in the direction of Spalding.

Sometimes towns paid for tramps to go away, although they did not like to advertise this fact in case it brought an influx of those keen to be sent on a journey. Spalding, for example, had trouble with two women and their five children in January 1855. They were given 'tickets' to pay for lodgings in the town but behaved so badly that they were put in the town's 'lock-up' instead. On being released the next morning, they were instructed to leave the town and — in the discreet words of the *Chronicle* — 'given the means to do so.'

Punishments could be harsher for men. Three men caught begging at Little Gonerby in January 1874 were sentenced to a month's hard labour each. The following month a tramp named John Knight got himself accommodation in Grantham workhouse but responded to this hospitality by breaking 24 panes of glass in the vagrants' bathroom; he also received a month's hard labour.

In July 1893 foundryman Charles Laughton came to Sleaford while 'on the tramp.' He started going from house to house in West Banks, asking for money or food. Unfortunately for Laughton, he was spotted by PC Green who attempted to arrest him. Laughton ran off, and Green chased him to Grantham Road where the exhausted tramp threw himself on the ground and said that if Green wanted to arrest him he would have to carry him to the cells.

Green hailed a passing cart and managed to get Laughton into it, but the tramp then lost his temper and smashed the constable's helmet. He was given three weeks' hard labour for begging and the same for assault.

Less blameworthy were those who fell foul of the law because of their poverty but without real criminal intent. In June 1847 the Carlton Scroop parish surveyor of roads issued a summons against Joseph Jordan for obstructing the roads. Jordan said that he and his family had been turned out of their house in May 1847 as they owed 26*s.* in rent and had set up a tent at the roadside. He had compounded his offence by lighting a fire at the roadside.

The magistrates listened to the case carefully. Jordan told them he would happily go anywhere, even to Folkingham gaol. It was also reported that the parish authorities had an empty house but would not let Jordan have it although he had five children. The court disliked the attitude of the surveyor, but still fined Jordan 1*s.* with 11*s.* 6*d.* expenses. They made no comment as to how he was expected to pay this.

For a poor man who had a parish cottage, all troubles were not over. In May 1841 a warrant was issued for the eviction of Jonathan Appleby from one of the parish cottages at Dunholme near Lincoln. The warrant was issued to the Welton constable, Coney, and the Inspector of Police, Ashton. But Appleby knew what was happening, and barricaded the house. He called out, 'No, you shall not come in. The first man who comes in shall be a dead man.'

The police brought a crowbar into service, and Coney rushed into the house, pinioning Appleby's arms down while Ashton wrenched a pistol out of his fingers, causing it to fire accidentally. Neither of them had reckoned with Mrs Appleby, who struck Ashton with a hatchet though with no serious effect. Thus two more people were made homeless.

Also homeless was John Hawsley who was arrested at Great Hale in July 1893. He was charged with an arcane offence, 'sleeping in an outhouse,' which was a form of vagrancy. Hawsley offered no defence other than that he was 'homeless and friendless.' He was given two weeks of hard labour.

Sir John Gilbert, A.R.A.]   [G. P. Nicholls.

'A common incident of blighted life:
Mourn for the wretched sufferers—child and wife.'

A. Elmore, R.A.]   [Dalziel Brothers.

'With memories black of many a bitter blow,
Dealt when the father's soul was dark with gin.'

CHAPTER EIGHT:
LOVE, LUST AND FAMILY LIFE

1. Child Murder

One of the saddest aspects of Victorian crime is the frequency with which the charge of murdering a child was made against a young woman. Also common, and generally in tandem with child murder, was the crime of concealing a birth. Behind these crimes lay the true picture of Victorian moral hypocrisy for, despite the supposed strength of 'Victorian values,' the whole of society was riddled with the most appalling standards.

It is generally supposed that the Victorians somehow disapproved of sexual activity. Certainly the public attitude of the middle classes at least could be seen as prudish, but beneath the surface a wholly different culture existed. Prostitution was rife, in both rural and urban districts. To have a baby out of wedlock was considered disgraceful and could lead to all sorts of penalties: the Poor Law authorities pursued errant parents and 'bastardy orders' were often issued. Often the saddest figures of all were servant girls, who endured long working hours and little opportunity for a social life: they also had to cope with sexual pressures from male employers. To refuse an advance could result in dismissal, to accept them could result in pregnancy... and dismissal. For such girls pregnancy could lead to economic disaster, but for unmarried 'respectable' women it could result in social disgrace and ostracisation.

Not surprisingly, therefore, in an age when abortion was illegal and contraception not readily available, a number of unwanted babies met unfortunate ends. Maria Andrew, aged 24, was a servant at the Talbot Inn at Holbeach and seems to have managed to give birth to a child on 29th October 1839 without anyone else realising. However, the following night she complained of feeling ill and went to her room. The girl with whom she shared the room suspected that Maria had had a baby and a search was made. The dead child was found between the bed and the mattress. Despite this, there was no evidence to prove that the child was alive when born and so she was found guilty of the lesser offence of concealing a birth with a sentence of only one month in prison.

In July 1851 a box was found in the churchyard at St Peter's, Eastgate, Lincoln by a boy who was playing there. It contained the body of a child which was inspected by a doctor; he was of the opinion that the child had been born alive, but there were no marks suggesting it had met a violent death.

Reports of the discovery reached the ears of Mrs Lilburn, a policeman's wife who also did various jobs in the realm of midwifery. She remembered a visit she had had from a mature woman who had asked to have her breasts 'drawn'; Mrs Lilburn was aware that the woman must have given birth recently and had questioned her visitor, but the lady said that she was married to a hawker and was on a business visit from Newark and had left her baby there with an old midwife.

When the woman returned to Mrs Lilburn's for a second appointment, she was followed home by some of the midwife's neighbours. They discovered that she was 39-year-old Sarah Thacker, who lived at Newland but was the daughter of a respectable Canwick farmer. She was unmarried, but admitted to having had a baby which she said she had thrown down the privy. No child was found in the privy and she was arrested.

Cases such as Sarah Thacker's were often treated very leniently by courts. In her case there was no real evidence to prove that she had killed the child wilfully, but she had 'concealed the birth' by failing to register the child. She was given six weeks' hard labour at the Assizes.

The same Assize dealt with another child murder offence, this one resulting in a nine month sentence on the lesser charge of concealing the birth. The girl involved was Maria Tasker, a 19-year-old servant at the Manor House in West Ashby. On 26th March 1851 she complained of feeling very ill at about 1pm, and was sent to bed; she was dosed with 'sal volatile.' At about 4pm the housekeeper went to see her and Maria said she was feeling 'much better,' but the older woman was suspicious and asked the girl if she was in labour, which she denied.

At about 8pm the housekeeper visited her again and noticed blood on the floor. She asked Maria if she had had a child, but again she denied it. However, at 9pm the housemaid went up to the room and found a dead child under the bed, with its throat cut. Although this would seem fairly clear evidence that Maria had murdered the baby, there was the opportunity here for legal casuistry. For a murder verdict to be brought in, it had to be proved that the baby had drawn breath after birth, which in the case of Maria's baby could not be proved as there were no other witnesses.

In September 1861 the Reverend Richards of Holbeach employed a new cook, Sarah Evans. On 4th October, Sarah complained of feeling ill and went up to her room. Later the family nursemaid went up to see her, finding her in bed but apparently fairly well. There was one strange thing: the carpet was rolled up and from it came a strange noise.

The carpet had been rolled up to conceal bloodstains and the baby, so it was not long before the whole household realised that the cook had given birth. Her room was searched and the baby was found in a box under the bed. It was still alive, but had gone dark in the face and it was discovered that a cord from Sarah Evans' drawers had been tied around its throat. Maria Clayton cut the cord but it was too late to save the baby. Evans was given ten years' penal servitude for murder.

To assist in the concealment of a birth was also a criminal offence. Maria Dowman was an 18-year-old servant at Normanby-le-Wold. She went into labour in December 1867. On 30th December she gave birth and disposed of the child with her mother's help. They were each given three months in prison.

In March 1874 servant Emma Wilkinson was found guilty of actually murdering her illegitimate baby on 7th December 1873. She received a lenient sentence of eight months' hard labour.

Another servant who got into difficulties was Ann Warner, who worked for Edward Cupit at the 'Roebuck Inn' at Stamford. On 23rd March 1884, 22-year-old Warner felt unwell but managed to do most of her work before going up to her room. The landlady became suspicious and went up to see her; looking in an earthenware jug, she found the body of a baby and a pair of scissors. Ann Warner told Mrs Cupit: 'The child is mine and I have not done anything to it.' However a medical inspection revealed about a dozen punctures and lacerations to the child's body.

Again the charge of murder was not brought successfully. For it to apply, proof had to be given that the baby had had 'a separate and complete existence.' Instead, Ann Warner was given a year's hard labour for attempting to conceal a birth.

Sometimes an illegitimate child became something of a millstone to its mother. Hannah Wright of Lincoln was an unmarried servant when she had a baby in November 1893. However, she found a childminder (or 'babyfarmer') to look after it, but resented the fees she had to pay. By August 1895 Wright had received an offer of marriage and decided that the child was a handicap. She told the child-minder that she had found a cheaper place for the child, but on 26th August she drowned it in the Fossdyke. She was found guilty of murder.

To end this section, it is worth considering that the law seemed to differentiate quite markedly between the death of a new-born baby and the death of a child. On 2nd August 1844 Eliza Joyce of Boston was executed at Lincoln by hangman Calcraft for having poisoned one of her own children. The motive for the crime was that she was afraid of having a large family, which reflects the desperation of the poor in the 1840s. Her sentence caused great interest and concern, for she was the first woman to be executed in Lincoln for 27 years.

She was due to be executed in public at noon, and approached the platform carrying a prayer book and dressed in black. The crowd, usually boisterous, was unusually sombre and still. The scene was described by a reporter:

> When about midway onto the platform she paused for a second and turned to take a parting glance at the scenery by which she was surrounded, as if to bid a lingering farewell to the bright world which she had sacrificed. Her face and features wore an aspect of ghastly agony...

Abortion was totally illegal in Victorian times and was regarded as being as serious as child murder, if not more so. This can be seen from the sentences handed out on the rare occasions when someone was arrested for having an abortion or helping to procure one. In 1876 Thomas Walker was a ratcatcher from Holbeach and he had formed an 'intimate' relationship with a widow named Lucretia Holland who worked at the Horse & Groom. In November that year she told him that nature had taken its course and she was 'in the family way.' Walker promised to 'set her right' and gave her some white powder to take; this was strychnine which he had obtained from the chemist as part of his work. The powder made Mrs Holland feel very ill and she sent Walker back out to get an emetic, but he did not return. He was arrested for attempting to cause an abortion and sentenced to 15 years' penal servitude; it is worth comparing this sentence to those handed out for child murder.

On a related theme were those parents who deliberately neglected their children, causing them to die. Martha Saville of Gainsborough starved her two-month-old baby to death in 1895, but was sentenced to only six months in prison. Of course there were also many instances of cruelty towards children, such as that committed by Harriet Pallander of Leake on her ten-year-old illegitimate child in 1854. The child tried to commit suicide in a local dyke after being hit on the head with a poker and having its toes and feet beaten with a hammer. So great was the suffering that the child ran away to the workhouse and Miss Pallander was sentenced to three months' hard labour by Spilsby magistrates.

2. Love and Marriage

Middle-class Victorian attitudes declared that marriage was a sacred institution to be treated with great solemnity and formality. For the lower classes it was often much more informal, not to say even chaotic in its planning and execution. Many couples moved in and out of 'marriage,' especially in urban areas, with no actual ceremony at all, while the pressures of poverty exerted a damning influence on many relationships.

Thomas Hardy's novel *The Mayor of Casterbridge*, was based around an incident of a man selling his wife. Such scenes were fairly regular occurences around Stamford in the 1820s (there are several references in *The Stamford Mercury*) and could have been witnessed in Lincolnshire until the 1840s and 1850s, though it was rare for a record to have been made. However, Samuel Sawyer committed an offence by having his wife 'exposed for sale' at a Nettleham public house in 1851. The couple had only been married for nine months when Sawyer dragged his wife out of bed, put a halter round her neck, and took her to the pub. A farmer named Proctor volunteered to act as auctioneer and the first bid was half a gallon of ale. The blacksmith bid 5s. but was topped by the miller offering 10s. The clerk of the parish, who should have known better, offered a sovereign. However, the wife failed to reach her 'reserve price' of 30s. and so was taken home again.

In late 1853 a poor labourer at Moulton sold his wife for 6d. to a man she had been living with. He was told by friends that such a 'sale' was not legal as he had not gone about it in the right way. So he put a halter on her and took her to the market at Holbeach, where she was 'sold' for a second time.

A frequent problem was that of the husband who abandoned his wife and children. Apart from the humanitarian aspects, this was a serious offence for it might result in the abandoned children becoming a liability on the ratepayers. In early 1855 the parish overseers at Stickford brought a case against Charles Dennis, whom they accused of having absconded, leaving his wife as a burden on the parish rates. Dennis complained that they had got married seven years before but after a month of marital bliss she had abandoned him, living as a prostitute instead. The magistrates sympathised with Dennis but, as divorce was not available to the poor, she was still his wife and so he must be guilty. He was sent to prison, thus ensuring that both remained a burden on the rate payers.

Of course there were many cases that reached the courts of violence between a husband and a wife. For example, in July 1868 George Chambers of Grantham had a row with his wife Ann after she refused to do what he considered to be her domestic duties. He 'blacked her eyes' and was arrested for assault. Given the choice of a 2s. 6d. fine or two weeks in prison, he chose the latter. No doubt Ann enjoyed a few days' peace and quiet.

Bigamy was quite common during the Victorian era. It was made possible by a slackness in registration methods and the considerable confusion that resulted in the working classes as a result of frequent migration. In 1854 Edwin Cunnington married his first wife, Susan, at St Michael's Stamford. The couple had four children, but in 1869 Cunnington left for Yorkshire and never came back. He made a new life at Idle, near Bradford, calling himself John Jackson and saying that he came from Northamptonshire. In this guise he wooed Mary Stead, persuading her to marry him in February 1870. This bigamy was discovered and Cunnington was arrested, his new 'wife' promptly abandoning him. He said, 'I've done wrong and I must make the best of it.' He was given a year in prison to encourage this penitence. At the same Assize Samuel Durant was given ten months for bigamy after marriages at Nottingham in 1861 and Lincoln in 1873.

Sometimes the punishment handed out for bigamy was very light. John Mellors, guilty of bigamy at Haxey in 1866, was sentenced to only two weeks in gaol. Elizabeth Hill of Weston St Mary, a rare example of a woman arrested for bigamy, was sentenced to two months in prison in 1877; the light sentence was partly due to the cruelty of her first husband, a farmer.

Two weeks' prison was also the sentence given to a Gainsborough nurse, Ruth Taylor, who married John Gibson on 20th April 1895 although her first husband, Charles Taylor, was still alive. She had married Taylor in 1891 while living in Sheffield but he had been a cruel husband, drinking too much and having fits of bad temper. He abandoned her for long periods while playing organ with an Italian band, and before going away would sell all the furniture so that his wife had nothing but an empty house. In 1893 he went off for good, leaving Ruth utterly destitute. She had decided to leave Sheffield and walked, eventually being found near death at the roadside on the approaches to Gainsborough.

Ruth Taylor was taken to the Gainsborough workhouse and recovered quickly. She was able to get work as a charwoman and then as a nurse. After two years in the town she was able to get married, no-one knowing about her previous life, but enjoyed only a few weeks of happiness before her first husband suddenly turned up. Finding her 'married' again, he told the police. Hers is a sad story and reflects the problems that many of the poor had to endure as divorce could only be obtained by the rich.

Although it was a civil rather than a criminal offence, 'breach of promise' is well worth consideration as it was so peculiarly Victorian. During this period marriage was often arranged by the bourgeoisie and the aristocracy as part of an economic bargain, and a 'good marriage' was as valuable as the grandest of houses. When good arrangements fell apart at the last hurdle, it was therefore tempting to seek legal redress: damages.

Mary Lester and William Tomlinson had grown up as neighbours at North Kelsey in the 1830s. In about 1834, when Mary was 19 and William 21, they became 'attached.' Mary had some 'property' of her own, £250, and in 1838 her mother decided that she should go into service to prepare her for life as a farmer's wife. So she was sent off to look after her two bachelor uncles at Bishop Norton, where William Tomlinson came to visit her.

Her mother then arranged for her to go to work for a druggist at Brigg and it was in Brigg that Tomlinson bought a ring for Mary. Next she was sent to Boston, where she received a number of ardent love-letters:

> My love...I hope you will not forget your dear William Tomlinson at Kelsey as he is true and always will be... Remember me to be your most true and affectionate lover.

However, these words proved to be false, for in September 1838 Tomlinson suddenly broke off all links with his erstwhile sweetheart. Mary heard rumours that he was to marry a woman with 'thousands' and on 15th January 1839 Tomlinson married a Miss Popple, collecting a marriage portion of £1,000, rather more than the £250 Mary had to offer. Mary Lester took Tomlinson to court for breach of promise and collected damages of £150.

In 1855 the Blenkhorn family moved to Frieston near Caythorpe and set up a ladies' boarding school. The Blenkhorn females became friendly with the Minute family of Brandon Court and, in the fullness of time, young Master Minute (aged 20) proposed marriage to Eleanora Blenkhorn. The prospects for the match seemed excellent and it was believed that young Minute would be given the family's other farm at Court Lees as a marital home and to provide an income.

However, the young couple remained engaged but no more, and the years passed by. In 1872 they were still not married when the boarding school ran into financial problems, and the Blenkhorns were forced to move to Sheffield. With such pressing difficulties, they decided to bring a case against the Minute family for breach of promise. It was fairly clear to everyone that the Blenkhorns were regarded as not quite of the correct social level for the young Minute, who declared that his parents had banned the marriage on the grounds that Eleanora would be 'no use on a farm.' Eleanora was awarded damages of £600.

Occasionally there was a case involving a couple who could not wait to get married. Such a case occurred in 1895 at Stapleford where John Shipton, aged 25, was accused of abducting Dorothy Jackson whose age was given as 'under 18.' The charge specified that Jackson had taken her away without her father's consent and 'with unlawful intent.'

The girl was a servant on a farm where Shipton was a carter and on 17th July 1895, at three o'clock in the morning, they ran off together to

Newark station. Shipton had promised to marry the girl, given her a ring and told her that he had £75 saved up in Manchester. They went to the Lancashire city and spent the night together, but the next day Shipton abandoned her. He was arrested at Manchester Victoria station when collecting his luggage and sentenced to two years' hard labour.

3. Sexual Offences

Life could be very brutal in Victorian times and this included the whole area of sexual offences. However, punishments for rape and sexual assault were generally less severe than for many minor crimes of theft.

In the earlier part of the Victorian period the law afforded little protection for young girls, who could be exploited by older men. In July 1851 George Johnson, a hairdresser at Newland in Lincoln, persuaded an 11-year-old girl into his shop. He took 'indecent liberties' with her, which involved giving her hair combs, sitting her on his knee and kissing her. He promised her other treats if she returned. He was fined £2.

In October 1859 James Brown of Metheringham was charged with 'feloniously and carnally knowing and abusing' a girl whose age could only be put at between ten and twelve. However, the court only brought in a conviction on a lesser assault charge and Brown was sentenced to a mere month's hard labour.

The passing of several Criminal Law Amendment Acts introduced an effective 'age of consent' law that could be used to offer some protection even when girls submitted willingly to intercourse. This was needed as older men could coerce young girls in a variety of ways. In 1893 Benjamin Cowling (59) of Rowston near Metheringham was convicted of repeated criminal assaults on Hannah Wilson, who was under 13 years old. He was given 18 months' hard labour.

Many cases involved sad and confusing family circumstances which suggest a breakdown in supposedly 'Victorian' values. In July 1895 John Spafforth of Scunthorpe was convicted of criminal assault on Edith Stones, a girl under the age of 13. She was a ward of Spafforth's and the child of his wife, though he was not the father. He had used his position to take advantage of her.

Offences against boys were much less common. However, in November 1895 an 18 year-old Grimsby fisherman, William Cordiner, was charged with acts of gross indecency and brutally ill-using two lads who assisted on a fishing smack. The judge told Cordiner that he deserved penal servitude for life, but the maximum sentence permitted was two years' hard labour.

A case that provoked considerable interest involved a surgeon from Coningsby. It was alleged that in April 1895 John Carruthers committed an assault on Ada Stamper, who was only 15. The girl was a patient of Carruthers' and had also been 'in service' to him. They seem to have become very intimate and had been noticed walking and talking together late in the evenings. The offence was supposed to have happened when Ada visited Carruthers at his surgery to pay a bill. In the trial Carruthers admitted being 'very foolish' but denied that anything illegal had occurred, while the girl contradicted herself several times. The case was dismissed.

These cases were very difficult to prove. The Assize that heard the Carruthers case dealt with five cases of sexual assault or rape, at Coningsby, Whaplode, Little Hale, Deeping St James and North Owersby. In only the last case was a guilty verdict returned, but the guilty party was aged only 14 and was merely 'bound over' for the rape of a younger girl. At the following Assize, in November 1895, George Laxton of Long Bennington received a sentence of two years' hard labour for an assault although he had originally been charged with rape. The girl was a farm servant and Laxton a worker; when the farmer was away he locked her in the house and committed the offence. There was much argument, as usual, as to how far the girl had co-operated and whether she had told him she was 17 when in fact she was 15.

In the early Victorian period rape cases were often treated quite lightly, but in the middle of the era attitudes began to change and it became a noticeably more serious offence in the eyes of the law. One of the cases that helped to develop these views in Lincolnshire occurred at Grimsby on 13th May 1866. Sixteen-year-old Lucy Sizer was the victim of an assault by five young men aged between 16 and 25.

Lucy Sizer was a servant girl of apparently good character who went to the evening service at the chapel with her little sister on the day of the assault. On the way home the girls were stopped by a man named Crawford outside the Dock Offices. He grabbed at Lucy and began to pull her towards some railway waggons, putting a hand over her mouth when she began to scream. He tried to get rid of her sister by knocking her over and, when this failed, offered her money to go away.

Crawford dragged Lucy into a shed in the railway yard where he was joined by four other youths who each took part in the assault. One of the most amazing parts of the case is that a dock policeman was attracted by the noise, looked in the shed, and then went away again. After the assault two of the youths helped Lucy towards her home.

The girl was very ill for a while after the event and developed serious fits. However, she was able to identify one of her assailants as a man named White. He was arrested, and implicated the four others for fear of taking all the blame himself. At the trial the defence tried to blacken Lucy Sizer's character, alleging that she had got a job in Grimsby 'to obtain money for a certain purpose from the fisher lads.' One witness said that she 'submitted to his advances' in May 1865. Despite this argument, the jury found all five defendants guilty of rape and they were punished severely: Crawford, who initiated the assault, was given 15 years' penal servitude and the other four received six years each.

The Sizer case contrasts very sharply with the fate of a girl involved in a rape case at Lincoln in 1847. The girl was a sixteen-year-old servant who became involved with Thomas Sindall, at 37 a wealthy corn dealer. On the night of the supposed event, 21st May, the girl went out to buy drugs and it was reported that Sindall 'accosted' her. He asked if he could go for a walk with her, took her hand, and followed her home. According to the girl, the corn dealer offered to take her to a 'fine house' in Sleaford and promised her £30. She said that a struggle then took place in Baggeholme Lane and she fainted, following which Sindall raped her in a nearby field.

The next day the girl told her employer about what had happened and the law swung into action. Sindall was arrested, but as soon as the case came to court it began to fall apart. Evidence was produced to show that the girl had actually promised to meet Sindall rather than having been accosted by him and that they had been seen walking 'like sweethearts' by a local woman. The girl had also dropped a sovereign, an unusual amount for a simple domestic servant to be carrying. Sindall was found not guilty of rape but the case clearly revealed the temptations for a wealthy man and an attractive girl who was, apparently, trying to find her own way to a fortune.

Girls travelling alone were dangerously exposed to attack, especially if they had been somewhere where they might have attracted attention. In 1877 a girl from Little Ponton went to Grantham fair and left at about 5pm. She was either followed or met by two men who knew her, Arthur Holmes and Thomas Jackson. While she was walking home they stopped her, pushed her into a hovel and committed rape. The girl told her mother, who demanded £10 from the men or she would go to the police. The men refused to pay and argued that the girl was 'willing'. The prosecution case cannot have been helped by the mother's dubious behaviour. However, both men were sentenced to seven years of penal servitude.

Not all sexual assaults involved actual rape. In January 1855 Eliza Newman was at the Packet House beershop in Boston's Bargate where she met Ed McCann. He followed her outside and then threw her to the ground, kneeling on her stomach. Eliza must have feared for her honour, but McCann simply 'made use of a very beastly expression' and ran off. He was fined 5s.

There were also those who exposed themselves. John Hollands of Harmston appeared at the Kesteven Sessions in September 1859 on a charge of having 'wilfully, openly, lewdly and obscenely exposed his person in the public street... with intent to insult females.' He received a month's hard labour.

On 26th October 1859 a farmer from Claypole, J. S. Lee, got into a Midland Railway train at Lincoln while drunk. As the train passed through North Hykeham he exposed himself to the other passengers. He was given a month's hard labour for the exposure and fined £3 7s. for being drunk in a train.

On occasion, couples also took part in revealing activities in public places. In 1884 Frederick Paddison and Mary Abbott were arrested for 'committing a public annoyance' in Spring Gardens, Louth, for which they were each fined 5s.

Prostitution was very common in Victorian Britain both in urban and rural areas. In some large towns it was an endemic problem often related to alcohol abuse. The 'Salutation' in Stamford was notorious as a brothel. In Boston in February 1855 Mary English was charged with being drunk and disorderly, but it was clear from her case that she had really been arrested as a prostitute. She told the magistrates that her father had died when she was young and that her mother had married again to a fellow named Robinson who 'not only encouraged her in an iniquitous life, but forced [her] into the streets to gain an infamous living.' Miss English pleaded to be sent to the Female Penitent Home in Lincoln and the magistrates agreed to this, showing that they had some sympathy for her account of being coerced into infamy. Less desirous of help was Elizabeth Watson of Wilsford, who in 1877 was convicted of 'wandering abroad and behaving in an indecent manner' in Grantham Road, Sleaford.

However, punishment for this sort of offence could be remarkably small: Emma Thurston was fined only 5s. for soliciting at Spalding in the same year, showing that the actual importance the Victorians attached to such moral offences was fairly small.

That prostitution was far from being an exclusively urban occupation is shown by the case of Mary Pacy in 1839. Pacy was described by the *Lincolnshire Chronicle* as 'one of those dark beauties of easy virtue who vegetate in the rural districts.' Joseph Ranson was a labourer and family man who fell into her company after going into Louth to withdraw £20 from a savings bank. While in the town he went to a 'dram shop' and then a 'licquor vault' with Pacy, whom he apparently knew from when she had been to his village to do some farm work. After the licquor vault Ranson bought some mutton chops; then he went with Pacy to a room in a 'tom and jerry' in Walkergate.

By this stage Ranson was drunk and the precise details of what happened in that house of ill-repute cannot be stated, but when Ranson awoke from his stupor he found both girl and money missing. Pacy was soon apprehended, perhaps because she assumed that her victim's shame would be good protection. The money was found in her boot, but she alleged that it was actually her savings from farm work at Withcall, though the amounts matched exactly. However, Ranson refused to bring a prosecution due to his fears about the cost of a case and so Mary Pacy was convicted on only a charge of prostitution with a two month sentence.

Much prostitution was conducted on a part-time or informal basis by girls who wanted to increase their normal earnings or by women who had fallen temporarily into hard times. This was a dangerous process, for it was easy to slip further into criminal ways. In July 1862 Eliza Clarke (26) was arrested for stealing 10s. from a youth named Thomas Hopkinson at Saxilby. The young man went to a dancing party at a local hostelry where he met Clarke. They went back to a chaff house belonging to Hopkinson's employer, 'for an immoral purpose.. After the purpose had been pursued, Clarke took the young man's purse and 'helped herself to as much of its contents as she thought proper.' The sum she decided on was 10s., which Hopkinson claimed she had stolen from him. It is hard to decide who was the more naive, but the court acquitted Clarke on the theft charge.

The links between prostitution and theft were also emphasised in the 1868 arrest of two Cleethorpes prostitutes. On 17th August 1868 William Proctor hitched a lift on a cart going from Cleethorpes to Grimsby in the company of two men and two women. On the way one of the women put her arms around him, but one of the men warned Proctor that she was trying to rob him. At this point the other woman suddenly grabbed Proctor by the hair and, in his own words, 'leathered me as fast as she could, then hit me with an umbrella.'

The case caused great amusement in court with the picture of a rather foolish young man fighting off the wiles of two experienced ladies of the street. A witness caused laughter by stating that 'one of the prisoners seemed suddenly to fall in love with the prosecution.' Ann Smith was found guilty of theft and sent to prison for a year.

Most larger towns had well-known 'brothels' which attracted a variety of problems, but unwanted customers cannot often have been among them. In 1877 Martha Benson was running a brothel at Waterside North in Lincoln when lunchtime was disturbed by three soldiers and a civilian, who banged on the door and demanded 'lodgings.' The unwanted customers were told to go away and, when they refused, water was poured on them from an upstairs window in order to douse their passions. The 'customers' responded by breaking the windows, for which they were fined 1s. plus costs. The magistrates took the opportunity to reprimand Benson and her 'lover,' Corthorne, 'as to the immorality of their conduct.'

Sexual offences included any activity that involved an animal. Despite the supposed difficulty of catching such offenders, and of gathering evidence from the victims, convictions were surprisingly common though details were rarely given in press accounts. In March 1839 William Robinson of Spalding was found guilty of bestiality with a sheep and sentenced to 18 months' hard labour. On 13th September 1859 Thomas Bett of Potterhanworth, 'feloniously diabolically and against the order of nature' had a 'venereal affair' with 'a certain ewe sheep' which quite horrified the local magistrates. However, it was difficult to secure a conviction in such cases and George Wilkins of Bassingham, arrested for 'carnally knowing' a cow, escaped with only the shame of having his name in the newspaper.

Alfred Elmore, R.A.]   [F. Wentworth.

‘ Where are his wife and children—both he had ?
Go ask the parish paupers : one is mad.’

P. R. Morris.]   [G. P. Nicholls.

These are the sisters, mothers, daughters, wives :
Hopeful—yet doubtful—all may not be spent.'

CHAPTER NINE: FOOD AND DRINK

1. Alcohol

One piece of legislation shaped the pattern of alcohol consumption in Victorian Lincolnshire more than any other: the 1830 Beerhouses Act. This law made it much easier to establish an institution that sold alcohol, if, indeed, 'institution' was a correct word for a place that was often little more than someone's front room. However, the law encouraged the sale of cheap alcohol and per capita consumption increased right through until 1899 despite the efforts of the temperance movement.

It is hardly surprising, therefore, that alcohol featured in many crimes of the period. Indeed the Kirton-in-Lindsey magistrates were forced to conclude that 'the prevailing sin of this town, too much resembling other places, is that of drunkenness.'

Efforts were made to restrain alcoholic excesses through the powers of the Licensing Act, but this could be enforced only fitfully due to the strain it imposed on a rural police force. For a publican to get caught was often due to a combination of carelessness and bad luck, for the movements of the local constable were generally well known. Nonetheless, on 4th January 1855 George Newton and William Poole both managed to get caught out with their pubs open after 10pm on a Sunday.

The two men ran pubs in Little Gonerby where Constable Beckworth was on duty. At about midnight, Beckworth tried the door of Newton's pub and found it locked. However, he could hear voices inside and so peered through the steamy windows and saw drinks still being served. When his face was spotted, all the people ran upstairs, later arguing that this showed they were 'family friends.' Much the same scene was enacted at Poole's pub. Both men were fined 7s. 6d.

Publicans could be charged for a variety of other offences. In November 1859 John Baines of Swinderby was charged with serving 'short measures' and also with allowing dominoes to be played on his premises, presumably as the game was an opportunity for gambling. He was fined 18s. for the dominoes and 18s. 6d. for the short measures.

Licensing laws could be used against customers as well as publicans. In February 1877 Lincoln Police Inspector Wright noticed Ann Mitchell watching him in a suspicious manner. Aware that she was up to no good, he saw her disappear into the cellar of the Coach and Horses where he found her buying alcohol from the landlady. Cannily, both landlady and customer were questioned separately, one giving the collection of a newspaper as the excuse, the other saying it was for an onion. Mitchell was fined 5s. for being on licensed premises during prohibited hours.

A few days later the landlord of the Horn Inn at Messingham was charged for allowing drunkenness on his premises. This was the cue for an enlightening discussion on what exactly constituted 'being drunk,' the landlord observing that 'he did not consider a man drunk unless he was so bad that when he fell down he could not get up again.' This argument was not accepted and he was fined £1.

Drinkers were probably quite glad to see landlord John Willey of Kirton-in-Holland in the dock in February 1884. He was accused of adulterating his beer with salt, but put up a defence that the water he used contained natural salt (perhaps he used sea-water!). A chemist was called to give evidence but complained that the sample had been delivered to him by Superintendent Crawford in an old wine bottle with a loose cork. The magistrates had to dismiss the case due to the dubious 'evidence.'

Any court that met had a succession of drunkards through its doors. A week at Kesteven Quarter Sessions involved Robert Green for being drunk at Skellingthorpe in September 1858 and three men all drunk in Branston. Green was fined 5s., charged 6s. 6d. costs for the court clerk and another 3s. for the constable. The money was given to the churchwardens of Skellingthorpe to spend on the poor. The Branston men had to pay a fine of 5s. each and 8s. costs.

A variety of laws could be used to catch the drunkard. These included drunk driving and being 'drunk on a highway.' The former was used against Waddington miller John Timms in 1859, when the cart he was driving through Bracebridge wandered across the road and collided with a cart belonging to the Kesteven magistrates! He was fined 12s. 9d. The latter offence caught out Mary Giles of Gainsborough in March 1874.

Mary Giles was drinking in the Saxilby district and called in at the Sun Inn, where she was 'a nuisance.' She was ordered out by Sergeant Kirk but at about midnight he found her on the road near Broxholme, staggering. She told him that she was walking to Gainsborough, but she was in fact heading in the opposite direction. She then fell over in a field. At the court hearing Mary Giles claimed to have been 'pulled about' by the sergeant and some other men but was sentenced to a month's hard labour. A similar sort of 'traffic' offence was behind the arrest of Henry Pearson at 11pm on the night of 22nd June 1893. Pearson had had 'an extra tot or two' after taking his cattle to Ruskington, and fell asleep across the Fen footpath, nearly causing PC Theaker to trip over.

A Spilsby hawker, Meshach Godwin, also surprised a policeman when he was galloping along in his cart beside a fenland drain. He nearly ran over Sergeant Henson due to being completely drunk! Godwin was fined 10s.

A comment on morality is perhaps intended by the presence of the noose in this contemporary woodcut.

Drink could often lead to violence, sometimes with tragic consequences. On 10th May 1851 George Large was drinking at the Horse Shoe in Stamford. He was sitting with a good quart mug in front of him and invited three other men, named McGlen, Barnett and Farrall, to have a drink. Barnett expected to be treated to a quart too, but only got a pint, whereupon he picked a fight with his benefactor. To add to the entertainment, Barnett then started to fight with Farrall. While this was going on, McGlen struck Large on the head from behind, then kicked him onto the floor. The landlady came in and Large was found to be dying of brain damage. McGlen and Barnett were arrested for manslaughter but the latter was acquitted; McGlen was transported for seven years.

On 14th December 1861 a Mr Styles opened his new beer-house in Navenby and encountered the hazards of his trade immediately. That very evening three brothers named Almond started a fight in the yard and Styles called the police. This added to the fun and the brothers enjoyed attacking the constables, one of whom received a direct hit on the nose. The brothers got three months in prison.

This story shows that baiting the police was a popular post-drinking activity. In 1866 William Bradley had a night out in Grimsby on a 'spree.' At 11.45pm he was 'in riotous humour' in Victoria Street when he encountered PC Atkin, who advised him to go home. Bradley, however, challenged the constable to a fight for 5s. Atkin arrested the drunk quite easily and took him to the lock-up; his pockets were searched and two pounds of smuggled tobacco were found. He was fined 5s. for being drunk and 10s. for having the tobacco!

In June 1868 the landlady of the White Swan in Barton got into trouble when one of her customers started to smash the pots in a moment of drunken anger. She sent for the parish constable, William Houghton, to throw him out, but in the course of the ejection the PC was hit. William Ferriby was fined 10s. plus 14s. 6d. costs.

Sometimes drink led to other offences being discovered. In February 1877 William Richardson of Corporation Lane, Lincoln, was found drunk in Waterside North. In his pockets was found a falsified begging letter, claiming that he was collecting money in order to buy a pedlar's certificate. He had used the money to get drunk and still had 3s. 4d. left on him. He was sent to prison for a week.

2. Food

Many Victorians would have eaten contaminated or adulterated food on a regular basis without any real power to check on what they were buying. Legislation to protect the consumer was only introduced gradually during the later half of the nineteenth century, for example the Adulteration of Food Act in 1870, and before then attempts at prosecution were often unsuccessful. This was especially so in areas where many goods were bought from pedlars. In 1841 one was found to be selling salt mixed with chalk, but by the time this was discovered he could not be traced.

In December 1855 Lincoln was rocked by news that respectable local millers had been selling flour to local bakers that was adulterated with plaster of Paris. Fourteen flour bags were seized at Curtis' shop and a prosecution brought against J. Stevenson's mill, but samples that were tested proved to be in the clear. However, the case against Messrs East proved to be stronger and evidence was produced by Thomas Sharpe, who had worked for the company until the middle of November when he had left after a wages dispute. While at Easts' he had seen bags which he thought were plaster and from which he took samples; when he took up a new job at Market Rasen, Sharpe showed the samples to the local policeman.

The East case caused especial interest as 'old' Mr East had officially retired but had been looking after the mill while his son was ill. The old man was said to be 'utterly incapable of wronging any man' but the flour had attracted attention through its 'rough texture.' Easts' solicitor advised them to plead guilty and they were fined £10 each.

Bread and flour seem to have been especially prone to having dubious contents! Late in 1873 the Lincoln 'public analyser,' Dr Lowe, found that two bakers had been selling bread with alum in it. They were Edward Hill of Epworth, who was fined 5s. with 26s. 9d. costs, and John Twells.

More unpleasant still was the sale of unwholesome meat. In March 1866 Mr Fieldsen, a 'pig-jobber' from Market Rasen, was arrested for trying to sell a diseased carcase at a Lincoln butchery. The flesh was actually a greenish colour. Fieldsen was fined a paltry £1 as he had apparently been deceived into buying the meat himself.

In February 1877 a food inspector called at the premises of James Nicholson, a cowkeeper and milkman of Pipe Court, Lincoln. The inspector asked to buy a quart of milk but Nicholson refused to sell it to him, knowing that the man was an inspector. He was fined £1 1s. In November 1892 PC Ward bought some coffee from George Cooke, a grocer in Metheringham. The coffee was found to have been adulterated with 60% chicory and Cooke was fined £2 10s. But probably the most common offence of all was the adding of water to alcohol by publicans: so it was that in 1892 the King's Arms, Lincoln, was fined 15s. for selling whisky 5% below its proper proof level.

Market Rasen clearly had a tradition for bad meat. In 1847 local people had got up a petition to the magistrates complaining about the sale of bad meat in the town. Apparently meat prices there were higher than anywhere else in Lincolnshire and this encouraged butchers to dispose of their unwanted stocks to the local people at inflated prices. Magistrates ordered that the law should be kept and promised to act if it was broken again.

Steps were also taken to check that the weights and measures used by shopkeepers were accurate. There were only a few inspectors to cover the county, so their progress around could usually be traced by a rash of prosecutions in particular districts. Punishments were usually small fines though the amounts varied: in 1858 Lincoln baker Thomas Hibbert took his bakery cart out to North Hykeham without the correct weights and measures so was fined £1 12s. Robert Comins sold flour at Coleby in 1859 and cheated his customers by using 'light' weights; he was fined 5s.

Thomas Faed, R.A.]   [Dalziel Brothers.

'Hungry and footsore, and without a bed :
Starving—yet dare not touch the meat and bread.'

CHAPTER TEN: RIOT!

The streets and lanes of Lincolnshire were often fairly lawless during the Victorian age and there may have been occasions when law and order seemed to be breaking down entirely. However, the worst social disturbances occurred in the periods just before and just after the Victorian age, involving the Swing riots of 1830-1 and the industrial discontent of the Edwardian era, which culminated in a full-scale riot in Lincoln High Street.

Much of the social disorder of the Victorian period was motivated by drink rather than by social or economic grievance. An example can be found in the 'Beckingham Road rioters' who created chaos in the Gainsborough district in January 1839. These 'lawless bacchanalians' created trouble in Gainsborough on a Saturday night after a few drinks, then took to a boat and crossed the Trent to visit another pub on the road to Beckingham. However, when they arrived at this hostelry they found that everyone had gone to bed and that the landlord refused to get up again for their benefit.

For the hardened drinker, this sort of setback was not a serious obstacle. The gang simply smashed down the door and helped themselves to drinks in the bar. In fact they went further: they ate 'mine host's' bread and cheese, fried his bacon and even drank his milk. In the middle of this feast the Beckingham constable arrived with a force of weighty villagers and, after a skirmish, the rioters were captured. Seven of them were taken off to Retford where they were duly fined 14s. each.

These sorts of disturbances were frequent but easily quelled. The most serious forms of unrest, though, generally centred on more notorious events: elections! A close-fought or bitter election contest was always likely to spill over into actual violence, as much in Lincolnshire as in other towns around the country.

In the June 1841 election there was trouble at Lincoln when the crowds gathered to hear the nomination of candidates outside the National School. It was claimed that Mr Brogden had bribed one voter with 10s. to vote Tory, but Brogden denied it. At this point sensible ladies among the crowd began to withdraw, their departure being 'the signal for parties to climb over the barrier, which was broken down.' The following day it was declared that the election had been won by Sibthorp and Collett, Lincoln having the right to elect two MPs. Even after the declaration rivals paraded up and down the High Street. It ended in the inevitable when the 'radicals' decided to attack the Tory headquarters at the Monson Arms, a fierce battle being the result, with many 'missiles' launched.

Six years later hostilities were renewed. The supporters of a candidate named Seely were reported to have kidnapped men likely to vote for the opposition and it was said that 'doubtful' voters had been plied with drink until they were incapable of registering anything, let alone a vote. Colonel Sibthorp's flags were torn up and the poles used as staves. A granary in Newland was ransacked and things degenerated into a riot outside the Saracen's Head with several wounded being carried away. Collett's supporters burnt an effigy of Alderman Rudgard.

During 1862 the election violence centred on Grimsby where sixteen men were arrested and sent to the Assizes after a riot at the Yarborough Hotel on St Valentine's Day. The situation had been expected to be tense and it had been arranged for a detachment of Hull police to be sent to the town. Unfortunately some observers blamed the start of the riot on the arrival of these very police! A better explanation is probably that there was an organised campaign against the Liberal candidate, Heneage. Two voters named Smith were believed to have been brought from Liverpool in order to get them to vote, and a rumour circulated that they were being treated to veal and champagne at the Heneage headquarters, the Yarborough Hotel.

A crowd gathered outside the hotel which included the sisters of the two voters, who promised to 'tear their eyes out' if they voted Liberal. These women were, apparently, 'violent' and 'great blackguards.' As the crowd grew impatient its temper turned ugly and a violent assault was launched on the hotel. Sixteen policemen, who were meant to be guarding it, retreated. After order was restored, sixteen men were arrested; of these, four were given prison sentences of three months.

There were a number of other post-election disputes. Mr Heneage, who lost the election, alleged that the riot had been organised in a deliberate attempt to prevent his voters attending. A voter named Hopkin lost his job after voting against his employer's wishes; this was in the days before the Ballot Act entitled every man to vote in secret. Hopkin had a very unfortunate day on the election: the 'blue party' suspected that he had been bribed by the Liberals and so they took him to a pub and got him drunk, then bundled him on a train to London!

"DERE'S SOME ONE IN DE STYE WITH PIGGY."

The Tory canvasser hiding from rioters in the pigsty, from a contemporary
Lincolnshire satirical song!

The elections in February 1874 also produced some notorious
disturbances. A meeting at the Corn Exchange in Lincoln was addressed
by Colonel Chaplin of Blankney, but was disturbed by supporters of the
'Radical Party' who, according to the impeccably-Tory *Chronicle*, created
some 'disgraceful and un-English scenes.' Trestles were pulled from
underneath the speakers' platform so that it collapsed and the reporters'
table was stormed. Alderman Brogden, a leading local Liberal, climbed
onto what was left of the platform and denounced Conservatism.

The day of the poll, 2nd February, was a Monday and the authorities
prepared for 'mischief.' The 95th Regiment was brought in from
Manchester and many Special PCs sworn in. All this failed to sober the
crowds who, as darkness fell, began to kick lighted tar barrels around the
High Street and threw stones to smash the windows of hotels with
unwelcome political liaisons. The soldiers were held in readiness in the
Great Northern Hotel and the stable yard at the Great Northern station.
There was a large fight at the High Bridge after which two young men
made mock election 'speeches.' The crowd then gathered outside the
Saracen's Head Inn but were incited by two young men who dropped
bottles on them from the attic window of Mr Odling's drapery store,
which was in turn assaulted by bricks and 'very bad language.'

The windows of the hotel taproom were smashed at about 8.30pm and the magistrates came out of the hotel to warn the mob to disperse. They received a reply in the shape of a hail of missiles, one of which hit Mr Clayton in the chest. A lighted tar-barrel was then rolled up and used to set fire to the stable yard doors; the younger Mr Brogden tried to pull it away, but was set upon by the crowd. At this point the magistrates resorted to the Riot Act and the soldiers charged out with fixed bayonets at the time when the city appeared to be degenerating into anarchy.

PROTECTIONIST MEETING AT LINCOLN.—(SEE PRECEDING PAGE.)

Rowdy meetings were part of the political scene. Here a meeting in Lincoln degenerated into the violence common in the 1840s.
Illustrated London News (17th december 1849)

A number of charges were brought after all this. A man from Langworth, described as 'a raw-boned countryman,' still had a glass looted from the Great Northern Hotel in his pocket when he appeared before the magistrates. Five others were charged after a riot at the Lord Nelson Inn. Edward Johnson was given six months in prison after being seen breaking the windows of Odling's shop by no less a witness than the Sheriff of the City of Lincoln. Mary Pickworth was charged with 'inciting the mob with profane language.' Three lads of about fourteen years old were arrested for smashing the windows of the South Bar Lodge, which was the home of PC Kemshall, and were fined 25s. each.

There were also serious disturbances in Stamford on 3rd February 1874. Three men were arrested after a mob had gathered outside Hatfield's shop in the St Martin's district, while windows were also broken at the George Hotel and in Water Street, for which Henry Bullamore was arrested. A mob of about sixty boys damaged the Black Horse. These arrests led to some colourful appearances before the magistrates: the three men arrested at Hatfield's argued that the trouble was the fault of the Special PCs, who had spent the day drinking and made no effort to control the crowd. Despite this, each was fined £1. Bullamore got into trouble again as soon as he appeared before the magistrates as he annoyed them by 'frequently smiling in the most complacent manner.' He also 'at times volunteered remarks in order to assist the memories of parties who appeared on his behalf to prove an alibi.' Because of this, Bullamore received a heavier fine of £5; he greeted the news of this by shouting, 'Three cheers for Buzzard!' Police officers had to restrain him.

W. Cave Thomas.]   [F. Wentworth.

'No better men when sober: drunk, none worse.'

97

CHAPTER ELEVEN: UNUSUAL CRIMES

The crimes of an era repay careful study, as they tell the social historian a great deal about the problems of the age. They also reveal much of human nature, and this pattern is at its most evident when we look at crimes that would be considered rare or bizarre today but which provide an insight into the Victorian period.

An interesting feature is the frequency with which crimes involving animals occurred in Victorian Lincolnshire. This was at least partly due to the fact that many people lived in close proximity to animals and birds, whereas nowadays most people only have contact with the family pet. However, it is difficult to explain the crime of stealing rooks, which a Lincoln man attempted in May 1837. He was seen on a house roof trying to 'bag' some rooks, which were presumably fairly comatose, when he was spotted by a police officer. The policeman ordered the man to come down, which he did very speedily, by jumping off the roof onto the officer, then running away while the long arm of the law struggled to find its feet again.

In July 1893 Elijah Pell was summonsed on a murder charge: the murder of a cat. Pell, of Great Hale, was seen by a boy as he set his dog onto the cat of William Blackbarrat. The dog chased the cat into a drain and it became trapped in the water; Pell then stepped forward and finished it off with a hoe. Blackbarrat claimed the cat was worth £1 and that he should be paid this in damages, but the case was dismissed as no-one was able to produce the corpse of the cat to prove that it was dead.

In the later part of the 1800s cases of cruelty against animals were often brought through the RSPCA. In February 1877 two men from Metheringham were brought to court for working a horse with a collar that was cutting into its neck, causing a nasty wound. The owner of the horse was fined 25s. whilst his employee who had been working the horse had to pay the costs of 10s.

There were important laws governing the movement of animals during times of disease. On 19th February 1866 a Riseholme farmer, John Marshall, sent fourteen cattle to Saxilby station. The cattle were seen by Sergeant Danby, who decided to check if their movement was covered by the official documents needed when cattle plague was a problem. He spoke to the herdsmen who showed him papers authorising the movement of seventeen cows, but the Sergeant suspected that a '1' had been added in front of the '7'. In court Marshall admitted the offence and Rev Apthorp confirmed that he had authorised the movement of only seven cows. Marshall was fined £10.

Another set of rules governed questions of public and private health. Ever since 1830 towns had been encouraged to set up Boards of Health to regulate their own streets and additional impetus was given to this by the Health of Towns Act, 1848. The emphasis was usually placed on what was called 'the removal of nuisances', a nuisance being anything that was offensive and a threat to public health. Cases normally involved charging an offender for the removal of the nuisance: Lincoln victualler Thomas Pepper was charged £1 10s. in 1847. Rules also governed when you could move manure or 'nightsoil' around urban streets, for this was considered to be a noxious practice that could make delicate ladies wilt. In 1877 a Boston cowkeeper, Edward Wimpress, was fined 9s. for moving manure during prohibited hours. Thomas Mawer, the Horncastle 'scavenger,' was fined 12s. in 1884 for scattering 'nightsoil' (the contents of earth closets emptied at night) along the street.

One of the greatest causes of nuisance was the tannery and leather industry. These foul institutions could often be found in densely populated areas of major towns and in January 1862 the works of Samuel Roughton and George Mole caused a nuisance in the middle of Lincoln. The local Inspector of Nuisances found a 'noisome fluid' flowing from Messrs Sandalls' saddlery in Flaxengate. It came from a large tank that was being emptied by a hose, passing along Flaxengate in a torrent, 'the stench from which was most horrible.' From there it ran out into Silver Street. In court it was reported that this happened very frequently and that the water was used to wash the tan-bark out of leather. The two partners were fined 13s. and 10s. each.

The law was rather slack when it came to the regulation of medicine. Although legislation was introduced to stop people passing themselves off as a 'doctor,' more or less anybody could sell a 'patent medicine.' People often went to see 'wise women' in order to save the expense of a proper doctor, and occasionally this could prove fatal. In July 1855 a farmer named Careby from Kelsey's Bridge got a thorn in his arm and the wound became infected. He went to see Mrs Spikins, a local 'quack,' and she applied some of her 'infallible' salve. The arm became inflamed and Careby died 'in the greatest agony.' Mrs Spikins was arrested for manslaughter, it being alleged that her salve had killed the farmer;

however, the case was later dropped since it was clear that what had really killed the farmer was his failure to visit a proper doctor.

Later in the century compulsory vaccination against smallpox was introduced but many people refused to have their children vaccinated. Cases were often dealt with in large batches; at Lincoln in January 1884 eleven cases were each handed out a fine of 15s. In January 1874 a Sleaford butcher explained that he could not have his child vaccinated due to 'conscientious objection,' but he was fined £1.

One law that has now been abandoned is that which involved the criminal prosecution of anyone who attempted to commit suicide. This heaping of further troubles upon a person can have served no useful purpose. Magistrates often tried to deal with offenders in the most lenient manner, but were circumscribed by the set penalties under the law. In June 1893 Henry Phillips, only 19 years old, attempted to hang himself at Bourne; he was given a month in prison. Two years later another young man attempted suicide at Skegness and was sentenced to a year's hard labour; the magistrates commented that 'these offences were largely on the increase and sentences must be passed on people who tried to take their own lives.'

In January 1866 Joshua Hall of Coningsby was charged with attempting suicide. The village constable had arrived to arrest him on another charge and Hall went upstairs to 'get his shirt.' As he took a long time his son went up to fetch him and found Hall with blood pouring from his throat. It was claimed he had attempted suicide but no evidence could be produced to counteract his defence that an accident had taken place.

Religion occasionally brought people into court as well. During the 1880s the Salvation Army developed rapidly in many areas of the country but often found its progress obstructed by unfriendly magistrates and hired mobs. In 1883 to 1884 there was quite a struggle in Market Rasen, where the magistrates objected to the Salvationists holding their meetings in the street. Captain George Noyce, the leader in Market Rasen, was sent to Lincoln prison for obstructing the street on a Saturday night. When he was released he was greeted by ecstatic supporters with a banner proclaiming 'Welcome Home for Jesus after 14 days' imprisonment.' A procession accompanied him through the town which included a religious chimney sweep on horseback, complete with brush in hand. At the market place, Noyce gave a speech and then everyone went to the 'barracks' in Willingham Road.

This incident contrasts with three Spalding youths who were taken to court for disturbing a clergyman during divine service. They were ordered to pay costs. At Owston church on New Year's Eve 1873, four young men behaved 'indecently' by hitting the tops of the pews with their hands and laughing loudly. They also threw wheat into the next pew and, to cap it all, Gervas Duffield was sick in church. However, the case against them was dismissed.

One of the strangest offences of all must have been that committed by five Grantham men who were charged with wilful damage to a field. In February 1884 they had gone to Wiseman's field and knocked some posts into the ground to form the goals for a football game. They were fined 1s. each. But even this prosecution is made to look worthwhile compared to that of Jane and Henry Stainfield of Branston, a few days before Christmas 1862. They were seen in Long Holt Plantation picking holly and were arrested for damaging holly trees. Fortunately the case against them was dismissed through lack of evidence.

On the Sunday of the Assize Trials, a special service was held at the Cathedral. This was one of the grandest events in the city's social calendar
Illustrated London News

REGULATIONS

AND

INSTRUCTIONS

FOR THE GUIDANCE OF THE

STAMFORD POLICE FORCE,

BY ORDER OF THE

WATCH COMMITTEE.

STAMFORD:

PRINTED BY JOHN FORD, RED LION SQUARE.

1857.

Even in the Victorian era, the powers of the police were strictly defined and limited. A rare pamphlet in the Phillips Collection at Stamford.

CHAPTER TWELVE:
POLICE AND PUNISHMENT

At the start of the Victorian era the policing of Lincolnshire was largely in the hands of amateurs. Parish constables were appointed for a year at a time and were unpaid; they had no proper training and the job was not a popular one. They had to report to the magistrates at each quarter session.

The idea that Peel initiated modern policing with his Metropolitan Police Act of 1829 is a false one. The Act had no effect outside London although the 1835 Municipal Corporations Act, passed by the Whigs, obliged all incorporated boroughs to set up police forces. This did not affect rural areas or the many market towns in Lincolnshire, although in 1836 the Holland authorities supported the idea of salaried constables, yet did nothing about it.

The next step forward was encouraged by the County Police Acts of 1839 and 1840 which were meant to stimulate rural areas to form police forces but did not make it compulsory. In 1839 the Lindsey magistrates met at Market Rasen and decided in favour of paid parish constables but only the Holland authorities retained an interest in proper police forces. All Lincolnshire's magistrates met at Lincoln in 1840 and decided against a professional force because of its cost.

Further improvement of policing thus came in a fragmentary way and focussed upon the control of vagrancy by the appointing of constables and the building of 'lock-ups' in market towns to deter tramps from visiting them. In 1843 Gainsborough built a lock-up and appointed a full-time paid policeman to supervise it. Alford followed in 1844, Grimsby in 1845, and Horncastle and Brigg in 1847.

The continuation of the amateur system of parish constables had many drawbacks, one of the most obvious of which was that it was applied in an inconsistent and haphazard manner. As an example of this we can look at the behaviour of a farmer named Day, who in 1846 was parish constable at Waddington. Whilst in the pub, Day was spoken to by a labourer whom he owed 5s. Day was in a bad mood and locked handcuffs onto the man, and then left him.

The labourer was suffering from 'English cholera' but walked to Washingborough so that he could ask the magistrate, Mr Sibthorp, to release him. Sibthorp thought it was some sort of joke and sent him away. He had to walk back to Waddington and for the next three days was unable to feed himself. Eventually the labourer persuaded another magistrate, Major Ellison of Boultham, to help him; Ellison got the Bracebridge blacksmith to cut off the cuffs and then gave the man a good meal. Day was fined 20s. for this abuse of his powers.

PC Sindall, who served in Lincolnshire 1860-80
Lincolnshire Police Museum

The 1856 Rural Police Act compelled all authorities to set up police forces in county areas. This produced some debate in Lincolnshire, where there was jealousy between the three parts of the county. The result was a mongrel system indeed, one Chief Constable, Philip Bicknell, controlling three separate forces! The boroughs like Lincoln and Boston retained their own separate forces.

The existence of several different forces could cause problems, one of which was jealousy! In February 1874 Boston's Superintendent of Police, Mr Waghorn, complained that his pay was less than that of similar officials in other forces. The Superintendents at Lincoln and Doncaster both got £160 a year and a house, while Waghorn got only £130 and no house. His salary was increased to £150.

PC Nelson, who served in Lincolnshire 1874-99
Lincolnshire Police Museum

A career in the police was not a popular choice and Bicknell complained on several occasions about the quality of recruits. Perhaps this was because of the conditions of service: an officer would have to walk about ten miles a night, had no leave at all until 1861, and when not on duty had to be at home in case of trouble. Bicknell hoped to bring in men from agricultural backgrounds who would cope with pounding the long beats in rural areas; he wrote that 'they must be clean, active and intelligent, of good height and well-made.' However in 1864 he complained that many officers were 'totally unfit' for duty.

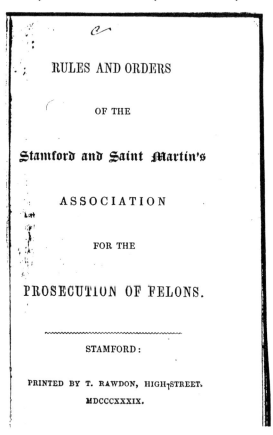

RULES AND ORDERS

OF THE

Stamford and Saint Martin's

ASSOCIATION

FOR THE

PROSECUTION OF FELONS.

STAMFORD:

PRINTED BY T. RAWDON, HIGH-STREET.

MDCCCXXXIX.

Victorian 'neighbourhood watch'. Such organisations were not uncommon. A similar one existed at Bourne. A rare pamphlet in the Phillips Collection at Stamford.

A lot of police time seems to have been spent dealing with very minor offences. In 1867, 522 beggars were arrested in Lincolnshire, while in 1893, 1,800 tramps were dealt with by the police! Police also had to transport criminals around the county, a practice that could be quite risky.

There were many escapes, for example in 1855 when PC Tooms was taking a thief from Market Rasen to Horncastle in a cart. The man managed to get his handcuffs off and then just leapt out of the cart and ran off.

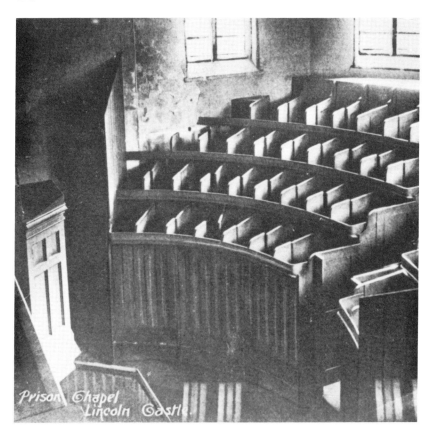

The Prison Chapel, Lincoln Castle
Lincolnshire Library Service

In the late eighteenth century a new county gaol was opened in Lincoln Castle, giving rise to some bad feeling among the magistrates of Kesteven and Holland who felt slighted by its location in Lindsey. The situation was not improved until the Gaol Sessions Act of 1824 provided a mechanism for administering gaols in 'divided' counties.

BEATING HEMP IN BRIDEWELL, AFTER HOGARTH.

Conditions in a women's 'bridewell'
— short stay accommodation for the criminal classes

The Prisons Act of 1835 tightened up on the standards expected of gaols and Lincoln prison was found wanting. New improvements were opened in 1847. The new Lincoln prison was opened in 1872.

The county gaol was supplemented by 'houses of correction' which were run by the divisions, for example at Kirton-in-Lindsey and at Folkingham. The warder of Kirton in 1845 was paid £45 a year, plus his rooms, coals, candles and a uniform. However, these jobs were not secure and some of the magistrates were quick to sack anyone who did not give satisfaction; in 1855 the matron and the schoolmaster at the county gaol were sacked, as the magistrates were 'not satisfied with their conduct.'

There were a number of escapes from the various prisons. Frederick Spicer was given two years in prison for embezzlement at the Assizes in March 1854. A few months later he escaped from the gaol and was eventually recaptured in London docks as he was about to set sail for Australia. He had succeeded in getting a job on the ship as an under-steward and was caught only because one of the passengers came from Lincoln and recognised him.

The 'House of Correction' at Folkingham, once the centre of
law enforcement in Kesteven

A famous escapee was Joseph Ralph who in 1854 was sentenced to
twenty years' transportation for burglary. He was first imprisoned in
Lincoln castle, from where he escaped in August 1854 by making up his
bed to look as though someone was still in it and somehow slipping away.
He then broke into a house and stole some silver but was recaptured at
Barton by two PCs, although he tried to fight them off with a knife.

By October he was back in Lincoln gaol and heavily laden with irons
to restrict his movements. However, he managed to take the clothes of
another convict named Baines, a lunatic responsible for a murder at
Crowland, and to make a key that would unfasten his irons from the wall.
Wrapping the irons in a blanket to stop them clinking, he scaled the castle
walls. He went to a pub at St Peter at Arches and got someone to remove
the irons.

When crossing the Trent Bridge at Nottingham, Ralph's appearance
made a policeman suspicious. When the officer asked who he was, Ralph
struck out but was taken into custody. At the police station he attacked

several officers with fire tongs but was subdued, and then packed off to Leeds gaol. He reappeared at Lincoln Assizes in March 1855 and was given an extra 18 months for cutting and wounding, and another 18 months in Lincoln Castle before being transported.

Former police headquarters in Lincoln

SOURCES AND ACKNOWLEDGMENTS

This book has been based upon many sources, but principally the following:

Lincolnshire Chronicle
Stamford Mercury
The Times
Illustrated London News
Thieves' Books for various parts of the County
Quarter Sessions records for the parts of Lincolnshire.

I am grateful to the staff of the following, who have assisted me at various stages of the project:

Lincolnshire Archives
Lincoln City Library, Local Studies Collection
Lincolnshire Police Headquarters
Museum of Lincolnshire Life.

Thanks are also due, on behalf of the publisher, to Philip Riley for proof-reading and to Stamford Town Council and the staff of Stamford Town Hall, curators of the Phillips Collection of Stamford publications, for their constantly helpful attitude towards our local titles.

INDEX OF PLACES